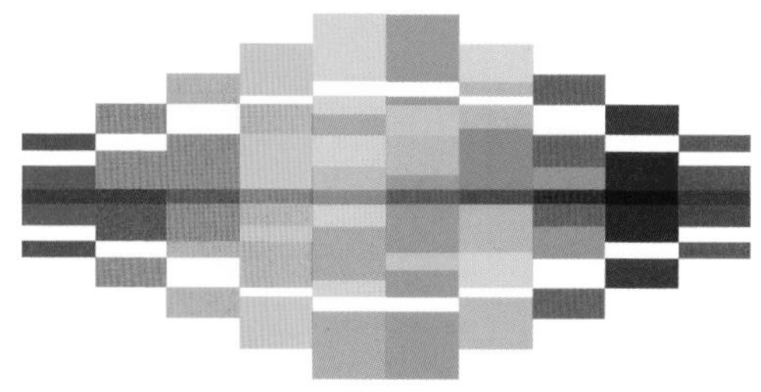

D0954151

FOOD & WINE

AMERICAN EXPRESS PUBLISHING CORPORATION, NEW YORK

FOOD & WINE COCKTAILS 2009

EDITOR **Kate Krader**
DEPUTY EDITORS **Jim Meehan, Joaquin Simo**
SENIOR EDITOR **Colleen McKinney**
COPY EDITOR **Lisa Leventer**
RESEARCHER **Janice Huang**
EDITORIAL ASSISTANT **Elyse Viner**

DESIGNER **Patricia Sanchez of Nice Kern, LLC**
PRODUCTION MANAGER **Matt Carson**
PARTY-FOOD RECIPE TESTER **Melissa Rubel**

PHOTOGRAPHER **Wendell T. Webber**
FOOD STYLIST **Alison Attenborough**
PROP STYLIST **Jessica Romm**

ON THE COVER **Mr. Stair (left), p. 137; Manhattan (center), p. 129; Summer Berry Fizz, p. 153**

AMERICAN EXPRESS PUBLISHING CORPORATION

PRESIDENT/C.E.O. **Ed Kelly**
S.V.P./CHIEF MARKETING OFFICER **Mark V. Stanich**
C.F.O./S.V.P./CORPORATE DEVELOPMENT & OPERATIONS **Paul B. Francis**
V.P./GENERAL MANAGERS **Frank Bland, Keith Strohmeier**
V.P., BOOKS & PRODUCTS/PUBLISHER **Marshall Corey**
DIRECTOR, BOOK PROGRAMS **Bruce Spanier**
SENIOR MARKETING MANAGER, BRANDED BOOKS **Eric Lucie**
ASSISTANT MARKETING MANAGER **Lizabeth Clark**
DIRECTOR OF FULFILLMENT & PREMIUM VALUE **Phil Black**
MANAGER OF CUSTOMER EXPERIENCE & PRODUCT DEVELOPMENT **Charles Graver**
DIRECTOR OF FINANCE **Thomas Noonan**
ASSOCIATE BUSINESS MANAGER **Desiree Bernardez**
OPERATIONS DIRECTOR (PREPRESS) **Rosalie Abatemarco Samat**
OPERATIONS DIRECTOR (MANUFACTURING) **Anthony White**

ISBN 978-1-60320-811-6
ISSN 1554-4354

FOOD & WINE MAGAZINE

S.V.P./EDITOR IN CHIEF **Dana Cowin**
CREATIVE DIRECTOR **Stephen Scoble**
MANAGING EDITOR **Mary Ellen Ward**
EXECUTIVE EDITOR **Pamela Kaufman**
EXECUTIVE FOOD EDITOR **Tina Ujlaki**

FEATURES
FEATURES EDITOR **Michelle Shih**
RESTAURANT EDITOR **Kate Krader**
SENIOR EDITOR **Christine Quinlan**
TRAVEL EDITOR **Jen Murphy**
STYLE EDITOR **Jessica Romm**
ASSOCIATE EDITOR **Ratha Tep**
ASSISTANT EDITORS **Alessandra Bulow, Kelly Snowden**

FOOD
SENIOR EDITOR **Kate Heddings**
ASSOCIATE EDITORS **Kristin Donnelly, Emily Kaiser**
TEST KITCHEN SUPERVISOR **Marcia Kiesel**
SENIOR RECIPE DEVELOPER **Grace Parisi**
SENIOR ASSOCIATE RECIPE DEVELOPER **Melissa Rubel**
KITCHEN ASSISTANT **Brian Malik**

WINE
WINE EDITOR **Ray Isle**
ASSISTANT EDITOR **Megan Krigbaum**

ART
ART DIRECTOR **Courtney Waddell Eckersley**
SENIOR DESIGNER **Michael Patti**
DESIGNER **James Maikowski**

PHOTO
DIRECTOR OF PHOTOGRAPHY **Fredrika Stjärne**
DEPUTY PHOTO EDITOR **Anthony LaSala**
PHOTO ASSISTANT **Rebecca Stepler**

PRODUCTION
PRODUCTION MANAGER **Matt Carson**
DESIGN/PRODUCTION ASSISTANT **Carl Hesler**

COPY & RESEARCH
COPY CHIEF **Michele Berkover Petry**
SENIOR COPY EDITOR **Ann Lien**
ASSISTANT RESEARCH EDITORS **John Mantia, Emily McKenna**

EDITORIAL BUSINESS COORDINATOR **Kerianne Hansen**

Published by American Express Publishing Corporation, 1120 Avenue of the Americas, New York, NY 10036
Manufactured in the United States of America

cocktails '09

FOOD & WINE
BOOKS

contents

Punky Monkey, p. 55

"Elina" glass by LSA from Lekker.

foreword

Compiling F&W's *Cocktails* is a great job: We scour the country for the best mixologists (we call it research) and then taste their drinks in our Test Kitchen (more research). This year, two star New York City bartenders were key in assembling the book: Jim Meehan of the speakeasy-esque PDT and Joaquin Simo of the elite Death & Co. Joaquin tirelessly shook, stirred or blended each cocktail here, and also created the terrific Latin Drinks chapter. Both men helped judge brands of gin, whiskey, vodka, tequila and rum for our first-ever taste test. They even helped by tasting the book's amazing party-food recipes, like the luscious Banger & Egg Sandwich (p. 189). To go with it, Joaquin mixed the Black Friar's Pint (p. 147), made with gin and spiced Guinness—it was all part of the research.

DANA COWIN
EDITOR IN CHIEF
FOOD & WINE MAGAZINE

KATE KRADER
EDITOR
FOOD & WINE COCKTAILS 2009

symbols guide

type of glass

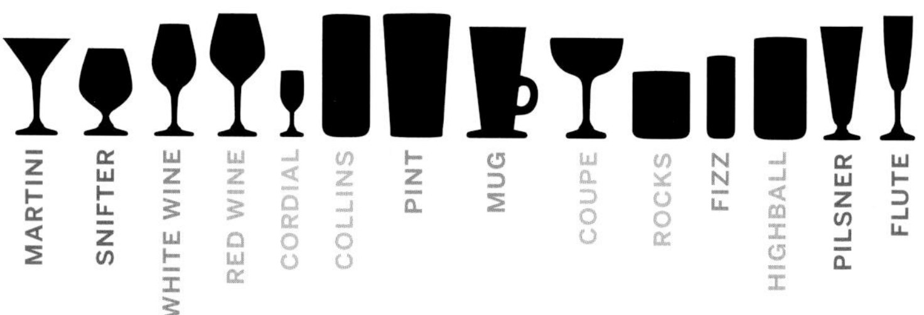

level of difficulty

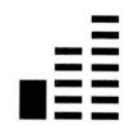

EASY
Simple to make, with ingredients that are readily available in stores.

MODERATE
Involve a little effort to shop for (specialty liquors or ingredients) or to prepare.

DIFFICULT
Require some drink-making experience or unusual ingredients.

type of party food

SNACKS
Hors d'oeuvres that are generally served in bowls, such as dips or nuts.

SMALL PLATES
Dishes that are ideal for sharing, like chicken wings or deviled eggs.

LARGE PLATES
Hearty dishes—burgers, calzones—that make great main courses.

type of alcohol

BRANDY
CALVADOS, COGNAC, EAU-DE-VIE, GRAPPA & PISCO

SPARKLING WINE
CHAMPAGNE & PROSECCO

BEER

SAKE

FORTIFIED WINE
LILLET, MADEIRA, MARSALA, PORT, SHERRY & VERMOUTH

TEQUILA

GIN

VODKA

LIQUEURS
GRAND MARNIER, NAVAN, PIMM'S NO. 1, SLOE GIN & OTHERS

WHISKEY
BOURBON, IRISH WHISKEY, RYE & SCOTCH

MEZCAL

WINE
RED & WHITE

RUM
WHITE & DARK RUMS, CACHAÇA & RHUM AGRICOLE

NO ALCOHOL
MOCKTAILS & PARTY FOOD

SYRUPS & PUREES

Watermelon-Honey-
Citrus Refresher, p. 83

"Vertical Paillettes" glass by Kim Seybert.

cocktail clinic

glassware arsenal

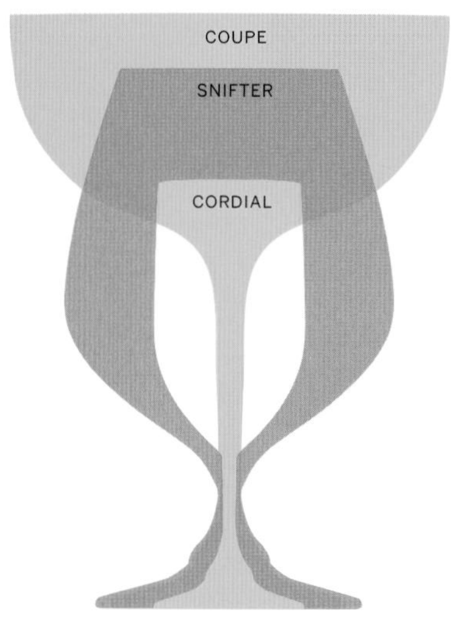

PINT
COLLINS
PILSNER
FLUTE

COUPE
A shallow, wide-mouthed glass primarily for small (a.k.a. short), potent cocktails.

SNIFTER
A wide-bowled glass for warm drinks, cocktails on ice and spirits served neat.

CORDIAL
A tulip-shaped glass for small, powerful drinks and dessert wines as well as liqueurs served neat.

PINT
A big, flared glass used for stirring or shaking drinks, or for serving oversize drinks.

COLLINS
A tall, narrow glass often used for drinks served on ice and topped with soda.

PILSNER
A thin, flared glass designed for beer. It's also useful for oversize cocktails or drinks with multiple garnishes.

FLUTE
A tall, slender, usually stemmed glass; its narrow shape helps keep cocktails that are topped with Champagne or sparkling wine effervescent.

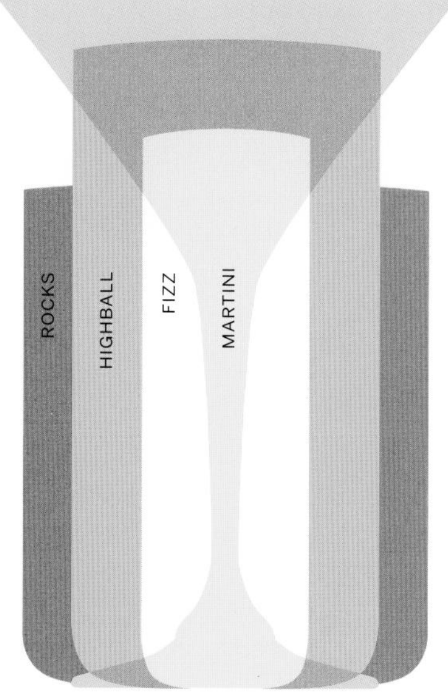

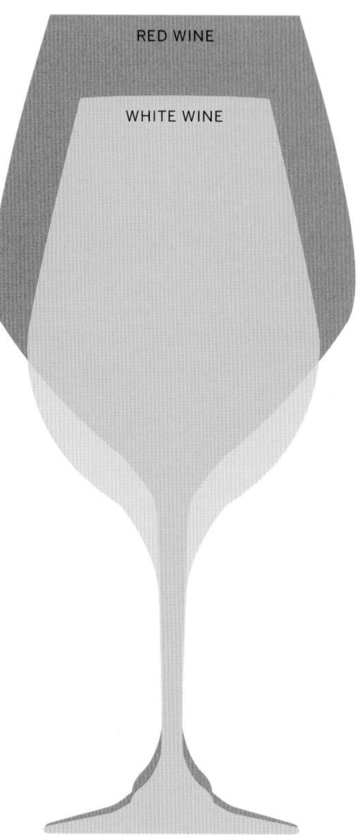

ROCKS
A short, wide-mouthed glass for spirits served neat and cocktails poured over ice.

HIGHBALL
A tall, narrow glass that helps preserve the fizz in drinks served with ice and soda.

FIZZ
A short, narrow glass for soda-topped drinks without ice. Also called a Delmonico or juice glass.

MARTINI
A stemmed glass with a cone-shaped bowl for cocktails that are served straight up (drinks that are chilled with ice before they're strained).

RED WINE
A balloon-shaped glass for fruity cocktails as well as punches. Stemless versions are fine stand-ins for snifters.

WHITE WINE
A tall, slightly rounded, stemmed glass for wine-based cocktails. White wine glasses are a fine substitute for highball glasses and are also good for frozen drinks.

indispensable home bar tools

BAR SPOON
A long-handled metal spoon that mixes cocktails without creating air bubbles. Also useful for measuring small amounts of liquid.

BOSTON SHAKER
The bartender's choice, consisting of a pint glass with a metal canister that covers the top of the glass to create a seal. Measure ingredients into the glass and shake with the metal half pointing away from you.

HAWTHORNE STRAINER
The best all-purpose strainer. A semicircular spring ensures a spill-proof fit on a shaker. Look for a tightly coiled spring, which keeps muddled fruit and herbs out of drinks.

MUDDLER
A sturdy tool that's used to crush herbs, sugar cubes and fresh fruit; it's traditionally made of wood. Choose a muddler that can reach the bottom of a cocktail shaker; in a pinch, substitute a long-handled wooden spoon.

CHANNEL KNIFE

A small, spoon-shaped knife with a metal tooth. Creates garnishes by turning citrus-fruit peels into long, thin twists.

COBBLER SHAKER

The most commonly used shaker, with a metal cup for mixing drinks with ice, a built-in strainer and a fitted top. There are generally two sizes of cobbler shakers: individual, for single servings, and large, for multiple drinks.

JULEP STRAINER

The preferred device for straining cocktails from a pint glass because it fits securely. Fine holes keep ice out of the drink.

JIGGER

A two-sided stainless steel measuring instrument for precise mixing. Look for one with ½- and 1-ounce cups. A shot glass with measurements works well, too.

WAITER'S CORKSCREW

A pocketknife-like tool with a bottle opener and a blade for cutting foil from wine caps. Bartenders prefer it to bulkier, more complicated corkscrews.

CITRUS JUICER

A shallow dish with a reaming cone, a spout and often a strainer that's used to separate juice from pulp.

mixology basics

rimming a glass

Bartenders often coat only half of the rim of a glass so there's a choice of sides to sip from.

1. Spread a few tablespoonfuls of salt (preferably kosher), sugar or other powdered or very finely crushed ingredient on a small plate.
2. Moisten the outer rim of the glass with a citrus-fruit wedge, water or a syrup or colorful liquid like pomegranate juice. Then roll the outer rim of the glass on the plate until lightly coated.
3. Hold the glass upside down and tap to release any excess.

making a twist

A twist adds concentrated citrus flavor from the peel's essential oils.

1. Use a sharp paring knife or vegetable peeler to cut a thin, oval, quarter-size disk of the peel, avoiding the pith (the white spongy part).
2. Gently grasp the outer edges skin side down between the thumb and two fingers and pinch the twist over the top of the drink.
3. Rub the peel around the rim of the glass, then drop it into the drink.

flaming a twist

Flaming a lemon or orange twist caramelizes the zest's essential oils.

1. Cut a thin, oval, quarter-size piece of peel with a bit of the pith intact.
2. Gently grasp the outer edges skin side down between the thumb and two fingers and hold the twist about 4 inches over the cocktail.
3. Hold a lit match over the drink an inch away from the twist—don't let the flame touch the peel—then pinch the edges of the twist sharply so that the citrus oil falls through the flame and into the drink.

double shaking

Cocktails made with eggs should be shaken well to emulsify them. Double shaking ensures the drink won't be overdiluted.

1. Add all ingredients—except ice or carbonated beverages—to the shaker and shake for 10 seconds (this is known as "dry shaking").
2. Add the ice to the shaker, then shake the drink again.

double straining

Drinks made with muddled fruit and herbs are sometimes double strained to remove tiny particles, so the cocktail is pristine and clear.

1. Place a very fine tea strainer over the serving glass.
2. Make the drink in a shaker, then set a Hawthorne strainer over the shaker and pour the drink through both strainers into the glass.

perfecting ice

Using the correct ice is key to a great drink. For most drinks, the bigger the pieces, the better. Large chunks of ice melt more slowly, and dilute drinks less. Detail-obsessed bars such as Little Branch in New York City cut their ice from large blocks. The exception to the big-ice rule: the crushed ice in juleps and swizzled drinks. Besides melting quickly, which dilutes potent drinks and makes them less overpowering, crushed ice also adds an appealing frost to glasses.

To make big chunks of ice for punch bowls, pour water into a large, shallow plastic container and freeze. To unmold, warm the bottom of the container in hot water.

To make crushed ice, cover cubes in a clean kitchen towel and pound with a hammer or rolling pin.

To make completely clear cubes, fill ice trays with hot filtered water.

To make perfectly square cubes, use flexible silicone Perfect Cube ice trays (available from surlatable.com).

top home bartending tips

Always use fresh ice, and plenty of it.

Don't be shy about the amount of ice you put in your shaker or mixing glass—you want to chill the drink as quickly as possible.

Never try to get juice from cold citrus.

It will yield up to a third less liquid than room-temperature fruit and require more effort. Let citrus sit at room temperature, or take cold fruits and soak them in really hot water for 5 minutes before juicing. Juices are best the day they're squeezed, but orange and grapefruit juices can be refrigerated overnight.

Drinks made with juices or egg whites require serious shaking.

Don't shake a cocktail halfheartedly for three seconds: Vigorously shake for at least 10 seconds to make drinks properly frothy. You shake a drink to wake it up, not put it to sleep. To make double-shaken drinks (p. 17) extra airy, remove the semicircular spring from your Hawthorne strainer (p. 14) and add it to the shaker with the ingredients before the first shaking. Remove the spring before you add ice (it could get caught in the coil).

Always refrigerate vermouth, sherry and other fortified wines.

Fortified wines that are left at room temperature might spoil. Buy the smallest bottles you need—most vermouths come in 375-ml versions (which won't monopolize your fridge) in addition to the larger 750-ml and liter sizes.

Chill pitcher drinks and punches with a large block of ice.

Small ice cubes will melt too quickly and dilute the drink. Ambitious cocktail-makers should also invest in a large (59-ounce) cocktail shaker (available from martinimartini.com) so they can shake large batches of drinks like margaritas for parties.

Stir—don't shake—cocktails that look best when they're clear.

Drinks that should be stirred are ones made with only spirits, liqueurs, bitters and/or syrups. The goal is to chill and dilute the drink with as little agitation as possible to avoid creating air bubbles that can cloud the liquid. To perfect your technique, practice stirring in an empty mixing glass with a cocktail spoon or chopstick.

make-your-own mixers

simple syrup

This bar staple is one of the most universal mixers, essential to many well-balanced cocktails. Stash a jar of the syrup in your refrigerator; it keeps for up to 1 month.

MAKES ABOUT 12 OUNCES
In a small saucepan, combine 1 cup water and 1 cup sugar. Bring the mixture to a boil over moderately high heat, stirring to dissolve the sugar, about 3 minutes. Let cool, then transfer the syrup to a jar, cover and refrigerate until ready to use.

rich simple syrup

Using demerara sugar gives this concentrated syrup a great molasses flavor. The syrup keeps for up to 1 month in the fridge.

MAKES ABOUT 8 OUNCES
In a small saucepan, combine 1 cup demerara sugar and ½ cup water. Bring to a boil over moderately high heat, stirring to dissolve the sugar, about 3 minutes. Let cool, transfer to a jar, cover and refrigerate.

easiest simple syrup

This extremely easy way to make simple syrup without a stove or saucepan is an old bartender's trick. The syrup keeps for up to 1 month in the fridge.

MAKES ABOUT 12 OUNCES
In a bottle or jar with a tight-fitting lid, combine 1 cup superfine sugar with 1 cup hot water and shake hard. Refrigerate until ready to use.

homemade grenadine

This lightly tangy, pomegranate-flavored mixer adds color and sweetness to drinks. For a tarter syrup, simply decrease the amount of sugar here by half. Refrigerate for up to 2 weeks.

MAKES ABOUT 16 OUNCES
In a saucepan, simmer 16 ounces unsweetened pomegranate juice with 1 cup plus 2 tablespoons sugar over moderate heat until thick enough to coat a spoon, 15 minutes. Add ⅛ teaspoon orange flower water. Transfer to a jar, cover and refrigerate.

conversion chart

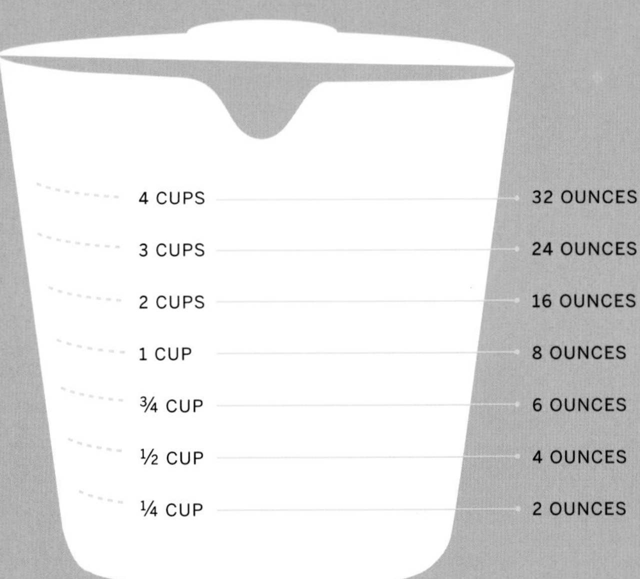

CUPS TO OUNCES

Cups	Ounces
4 CUPS	32 OUNCES
3 CUPS	24 OUNCES
2 CUPS	16 OUNCES
1 CUP	8 OUNCES
¾ CUP	6 OUNCES
½ CUP	4 OUNCES
¼ CUP	2 OUNCES

TABLESPOONS TO OUNCES

Tablespoons	Ounces
2 TABLESPOONS	1 OUNCE
1½ TABLESPOONS	¾ OUNCE
1 TABLESPOON	½ OUNCE
½ TABLESPOON	¼ OUNCE

spirits lexicon

These are many of the spirits, mixers and other cocktail ingredients in this book. They can be found at most liquor stores and online spirits retailers.

Spirits designated with a star (★) are mixologists' new favorites.

★ **Absinthe** An anise-flavored spirit banned in the United States in 1912 in part because its namesake ingredient, *Artemisia absinthium,* or wormwood, is known to be toxic in large doses. Absinthe containing acceptable amounts of wormwood is now available in the United States.

Agave nectar A sweet syrup made from the core of the cactus-like agave plant. It's thinner and dissolves more easily than honey.

Amaro A bittersweet Italian herbal liqueur often served as an after-dinner drink. **Montenegro amaro** has a spicy orange flavor. **Nonino Quintessentia amaro** is infused with herbs and aged in oak barrels for five years. **Meletti amaro** is also herb-infused; it has a floral aroma and a saffron flavor.

Angostura bitters A brand of concentrated aromatic bitters created in Angostura, Venezuela, in 1824 from a secret combination of herbs and spices.

★ **Aperol** A bitter orange Italian aperitif flavored with rhubarb and the gentian plant.

Apple brandy A distilled fermented apple cider that is aged in oak barrels and usually 80 to 90 proof. **Bonded apple brandy,** which is preferable in cocktails because of its powerful green-apple flavor, is 100 proof.

Applejack An American apple brandy often blended with neutral spirits.

Apricot brandy An often sweetened liqueur distilled from apricots.

Aquavit A clear grain- or potato-based spirit flavored with caraway seeds and other botanicals, such as fennel, anise and citrus peel.

Averna A bitter Italian liqueur flavored with herbs and citrus peel.

Bénédictine A brandy-based herbal liqueur derived from a recipe developed by French monks in 1510.

Bitters A superconcentrated solution of bitter and often aromatic plants that adds flavor and complexity to drinks. Varieties include orange, lemon, peach and aromatic bitters, the best known of which is **Angostura.** (See also **Fee Brothers bitters** and **Peychaud's bitters.**)

Cachaça A potent Brazilian spirit distilled from fresh sugarcane juice; some of the best versions are made in copper pot stills and aged in wooden casks.

Calvados A cask-aged brandy made in the Normandy region of France from apples and sometimes pears.

Campari A bright red bitter Italian aperitif made from herbs and fruit.

Carpano Antica Formula A rich and complex crimson-colored sweet Italian vermouth.

Chartreuse A spicy French liqueur made from 130 botanicals; **green** Chartreuse is more potent than the honey-sweetened **yellow** one.

Cognac An oak-aged distilled brandy made in the Cognac region of France. It's frequently served as an after-dinner drink.

Cointreau A distilled French triple sec that is flavored with the essential oils of sun-dried sweet and bitter orange peels.

Curaçao A general term for orange-flavored liqueurs produced in the Dutch West Indies.

★ **Cynar** A pleasantly bitter Italian liqueur made from 13 herbs and plants, including artichokes.

Drambuie A whiskey-based Scottish liqueur flavored with honey.

Eau-de-vie A clear, unaged fruit brandy. Varieties include **kirsch** (cherry), **framboise** (raspberry), **poire** (pear) and **mirabelle** (plum).

★ **Fee Brothers bitters** A brand of bitters made in Rochester, New York, for more than 60 years. Classic flavors include orange and peach; grapefruit is a newer flavor.

Fernet-Branca A bitter Italian digestif made from 27 herbs.

Grenadine A sweet red syrup made from pomegranate juice and sugar (see the Homemade Grenadine recipe on page 20).

Heering cherry liqueur A brandy-based Danish cherry liqueur.

Herbsaint An anise-flavored absinthe substitute produced in New Orleans.

Licor 43 A citrus-and-vanilla-flavored Spanish liqueur made from a combination of 43 herbs and spices.

★ **Lillet** A wine-based French aperitif flavored with orange peel and quinine. The rare **rouge** (red) variety is sweeter than the more widely available **blanc** (white).

Limoncello An Italian liqueur made from lemon peels soaked in neutral spirits, then sweetened with sugar.

★ **Maraschino liqueur** A clear Italian liqueur, the best of which is made from bittersweet marasca cherries and their pits, aged in ash barrels, then sweetened with sugar.

Marsala A Sicilian fortified wine; styles include **secco** (dry), which is often served as an aperitif, and **semisecco** (semisweet) and **dolce** (sweet), which are commonly served as dessert wines.

Mead A fermented honey-based beverage that is often flavored with herbs, spices or flowers.

★ **Mezcal** An agave-based spirit with a smoky flavor that comes from roasting the agave hearts in pits before fermentation. The best mezcal is made in Mexico's Oaxaca region.

Navan A Cognac infused with black Madagascar vanilla.

Orgeat A lightly sweet, nonalcoholic, almond-flavored syrup accented with orange flower water.

★ **Peychaud's bitters** A brand of bitters with bright anise and cranberry flavors; the recipe dates to 19th-century New Orleans.

Pimm's No. 1 A gin-based English aperitif often served with citrus-flavored soda or ginger beer.

Pisco A clear spirit distilled from grapes in the wine-producing regions of Peru and Chile. **Acholado** pisco is made from the juice and pulp of multiple grape varieties.

Poire Williams A pear eau-de-vie, usually made in Switzerland or the Alsace region of France.

Port A fortified wine from the Douro region of Portugal. Styles include fruity, young **ruby** ports; richer, nuttier **tawnies;** thick-textured, oak-aged **late bottled vintage** (LBV) versions; and decadent **vintage** ports, made from the best grapes in the best vintages.

Punt e Mes A spicy, orange-accented sweet vermouth fortified with bitters.

★ **Sherry** A fortified wine from Spain's Jerez region. Varieties include dry styles like **fino** and **manzanilla;** nuttier, richer **amontillados** and **olorosos;** and viscous sweet versions such as **cream sherry.** Sweet, nutty **East India sherry** falls somewhere between an oloroso and a cream sherry in style.

Sloe gin A bittersweet red liqueur with a nutty finish that comes from infusing a neutral spirit or gin with sloe berries and sugar.

St. Elizabeth Allspice Dram A brand of rum-based liqueur from Austria made with dried Jamaican allspice berries.

★ **St-Germain elderflower liqueur** A French brand of lightly floral liqueur with hints of pear, peach and grapefruit zest. It's made from macerated elderflower blossoms and eau-de-vie (grape spirit).

Triple sec An orange-flavored distilled neutral spirit that is similar to curaçao but not as sweet. Cointreau is the most famous brand of triple sec, created in France in 1875.

Velvet Falernum A low-alcohol, sugarcane-based liqueur from Barbados that's flavored with clove, almond and lime.

★ **Vermouth** An aromatic fortified wine. It can be white or red, and ranges from dry (used in martinis) to very sweet (often served as an aperitif). **Bianco vermouth** is an aromatic, sweet Italian white vermouth traditionally served on the rocks.

essential spirits

Gin is a clear spirit flavored predominantly with juniper berries and other botanicals like coriander, anise seed and lemon peel. These ingredients can give gin piney, spicy or citrusy notes. Ubiquitous dry gin, also known as **London dry,** is bolder in flavor than the slightly sweet, less botanically intense **Old Tom** style.

Vodka is often defined by what it doesn't have—aroma, taste or color. While usually made with fermented grains, vodka can be produced from nearly any fruit or vegetable that contains sugar, from grapes to beets. The finest flavored vodkas are often made with fruit-infused grain alcohol run through a pot still.

Tequila The best ones are made with 100 percent blue agave.
Blanco These unaged tequilas are earthy and peppery.
Reposado Reposado ("rested") tequilas sit for up to a year in casks, resulting in a mellow taste and golden color.
Mezcal Smoky, agave-based mezcal is a cousin of tequila.

Rye Somewhat spicy, rye whiskey is made with a minimum 51 percent rye; **straight rye whiskey** is aged for at least two years.
Scotch **Single malts,** unlike **blends,** come from only one distillery.
Bourbon Made primarily with corn and aged for a minimum of two years, bourbon tastes of warm brown sugar and toffee.

Rum Most are made with fermented and distilled molasses.
White These clear, usually dry rums typically age less than a year.
Dark Aged for five-plus years, dark rums have deep caramel flavor.
Rhum Agricole This aromatic rum is made in the French West Indies from fresh sugarcane juice.

taste-test winners

A panel of star mixologists and editors from FOOD & WINE Magazine tasted dozens of spirits to find these winners.

Black & Brown, p. 111

"Beaumont" glass by Theresienthal.

BEST whiskey

BOURBON

value	**Bulleit** Tom Bulleit's peppery bourbon is made according to his great-great-grandfather's 19th-century recipe.
high-end	**Booker's** This unfiltered Kentucky bourbon is bottled straight out of the barrel at an intense 126 proof.

RYE

value	**Wild Turkey** Jimmy Russell, a 55-year Wild Turkey veteran, distills this beautifully balanced rye whiskey.
high-end	**Sazerac 18-Year-Old** This rye is produced at one of America's oldest distilleries, operating since 1787.

SCOTCH

blended	**Black Bottle** Whiskies from seven distilleries on the Scottish island of Islay go into this peaty blend.
single-malt	**The Macallan** Macallan takes the oak casks it uses very seriously; all are handcrafted or hand-chosen.

best new u.s. whiskey

Stranahan's
This Colorado microdistillery makes whiskey with fermented barley custom-blended by a nearby brewery.

BEST gin

value — **Beefeater** Beefeater was the only gin on the *Queen Elizabeth 2* during her maiden voyage in 1969.

high-end — **Junípero** This full-bodied gin comes from Anchor Distilling, part of San Francisco's famed Anchor Brewing.

new — **Reisetbauer Blue Gin** Renowned for his eaux-de-vie, Hans Reisetbauer now produces this piney gin.

all-purpose — **Plymouth** Winston Churchill favored this well-balanced gin, made in England's oldest distillery.

mixing — **Bombay Sapphire** Ten botanicals, from juniper berry to the Cubeb berry, go into this clean-tasting gin.

BEST vodka

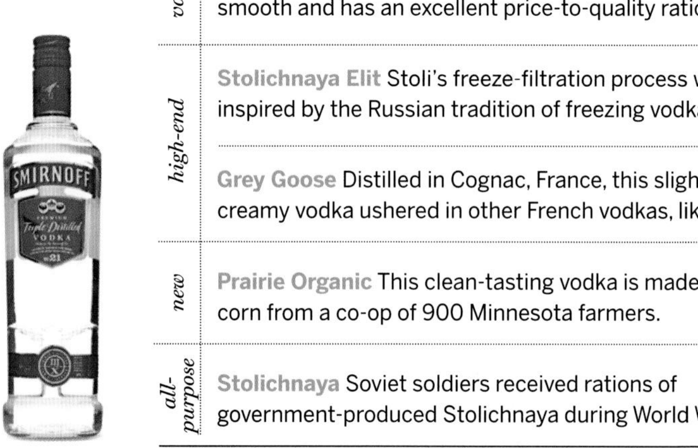

value — **Smirnoff** The world's top-selling vodka, Smirnoff is especially smooth and has an excellent price-to-quality ratio.

high-end — **Stolichnaya Elit** Stoli's freeze-filtration process was inspired by the Russian tradition of freezing vodka outdoors.

Grey Goose Distilled in Cognac, France, this slightly creamy vodka ushered in other French vodkas, like Cîroc.

new — **Prairie Organic** This clean-tasting vodka is made with corn from a co-op of 900 Minnesota farmers.

all-purpose — **Stolichnaya** Soviet soldiers received rations of government-produced Stolichnaya during World War II.

BEST tequila

blanco	**El Tesoro Platinum** El Tesoro's herbaceous tequila uses both the juice and pulp of the core of the blue agave.
reposado	**Siembra Azul** Instead of using electric steam ovens, Siembra Azul still roasts its agave in traditional clay ovens.
añejo	**Gran Centenario** A notorious product-placement deal landed this tequila in a Neil Simon Broadway production.
mezcal	**Los Amantes Joven** This unaged, small-batch mezcal has strong agave flavor and an assertive smokiness.
mixing	**Patrón** Each bottle of this tequila is individually numbered and handcrafted using recycled glass.

BEST rum

white	**Flor de Caña Extra Dry** Aged for four years—unusual for a white rum—this Nicaraguan export mixes well in daiquiris.
white	**10 Cane** Made from Trinidadian sugarcane, this wonderfully aromatic rum tastes of fruit and toffee.
dark	**Gosling's Black Seal** Bermuda's oldest business produces this rich, caramelly rum.
aged	**Ron Zacapa 23-Year-Old** This honey-inflected rum is aged in barrels previously used for bourbon and sherry.
rhum agricole	**Neisson Réserve Spéciale** Only sugarcane from the Neisson Martinique estate is used for this rum.

Okanagan, p. 36

"Pointe" Champagne coupe by Calvin Klein Home; "Baroque" skewer from Fitzsu.

APERITIFS

recipes by jamie boudreau

MEET THE MIXOLOGIST

jamie boudreau

Jamie Boudreau is known for eccentric ingredient combinations (bacon and bourbon) and cutting-edge techniques (injecting flavored egg whites with nitrous oxide to make foam). An all-around exceptional mixologist, he became adept at making predinner drinks while working at Vancouver's legendary restaurant Lumière (now run by Daniel Boulud). Boudreau is planning to open his own place soon.

bitter moon

This is a variation on a cocktail Boudreau created for Fat Bastard Wine using the company's Chardonnay. Campari and grapefruit juice give the drink a pleasantly bitter kick.

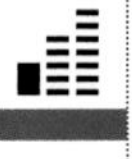

- Ice
- 2 ounces full-bodied white wine
- 1 ounce gin
- ¼ ounce Campari
- 2 ounces fresh grapefruit juice

Fill a cocktail shaker with ice. Add all of the remaining ingredients and shake well. Strain into a chilled martini glass.

châtelaine

Wine-tails (Boudreau's name for wine-based cocktails) are showing up at more and more bars. The light, fruity Châtelaine, made with white wine, also contains pomegranate juice, which is a noted antioxidant.

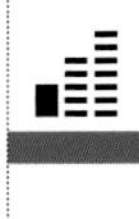

Ice
2 ounces crisp white wine
1 ounce gin
½ ounce St-Germain elderflower liqueur
1 ounce pomegranate juice

Fill a cocktail shaker with ice. Add all of the remaining ingredients and shake well. Strain the drink into a chilled martini glass.

l'amour en fuite

Boudreau came up with this fragrant drink after sampling a bottle of St-Germain, a recently released elderflower liqueur from France.

¼ ounce absinthe
Ice
1½ ounces gin
¾ ounce Lillet blanc
¼ ounce St-Germain elderflower liqueur

Rinse a chilled coupe with the absinthe, then pour it out. Fill a pint glass with ice. Add all of the remaining ingredients, stir well and strain into the coupe.

okanagan

This drink pays homage to the orchards and vineyards of British Columbia's fertile Okanagan Valley.

Ice

2 ounces Blueberry Cabernet Sauvignon (below)

1 ounce Calvados

½ ounce apricot liqueur

5 blueberries skewered on a pick, for garnish

Fill a pint glass with ice. Add all of the remaining ingredients except the skewered blueberries and stir well. Strain into a chilled coupe and garnish with the skewered blueberries.

blueberry cabernet sauvignon

In a jar, combine 10 ounces Cabernet Sauvignon with 4 blueberry-flavored tea bags. Let steep for 5 minutes, then squeeze the tea bags and discard. Cover the wine and refrigerate for up to 2 weeks. Makes 10 ounces.

asian peach

Daiginjo sake is known for its subtle peach notes. To amplify the peachy flavor in this drink, Boudreau adds muddled fresh fruit.

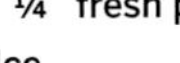

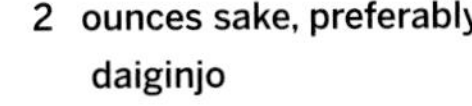

¼ fresh peach
Ice
2 ounces sake, preferably daiginjo
½ ounce gin
¼ ounce fresh lemon juice
¼ ounce Lemongrass Syrup (below)

In a cocktail shaker, muddle the peach. Add ice and the remaining ingredients and shake well. Double strain (p. 17) into a chilled coupe.

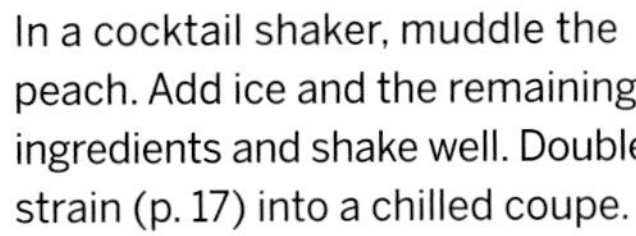

lemongrass syrup

In a small saucepan, bring 6 ounces Simple Syrup (p. 20) to a boil. Remove from the heat and add 1 coarsely chopped fresh lemongrass stalk. Let cool, then cover and refrigerate overnight. Strain the syrup into a jar, cover and refrigerate for up to 3 weeks. Makes 6 ounces.

Feng Shui

Champagne coupe from TableArt.

feng shui

The light, fragrant Feng Shui harmoniously combines flavors from around the world: lychee from southern China, sake from Japan, thyme from the Mediterranean and gin from Holland.

1 canned lychee, plus 1 lychee skewered on a pick for garnish
Ice
1 ounce sake
1 ounce gin
1 thyme sprig, plus 1 sprig for garnish
¼ ounce fresh lemon juice
¼ ounce Simple Syrup (p. 20)

In a cocktail shaker, muddle the lychee. Add ice and the remaining ingredients except the garnishes and shake well. Double strain (p. 17) into a chilled coupe; garnish with the skewered lychee and thyme sprig.

darb cocktail

Boudreau adapted this drink from Harry Craddock's 1930 Savoy Cocktail Book. *For the best flavor, he recommends using Rothman & Winter Orchard Apricot Liqueur or another high-quality apricot liqueur.*

Ice
¾ ounce gin
¾ ounce dry vermouth
¾ ounce apricot liqueur
¼ ounce fresh lemon juice

Fill a cocktail shaker with ice. Add all of the remaining ingredients and shake well. Strain the drink into a chilled coupe.

rosemary paloma

The Paloma is a refreshing Mexican tequila drink traditionally made with grapefruit soda. Boudreau substitutes grapefruit juice and club soda, and adds rosemary syrup to give the drink an herbal twist.

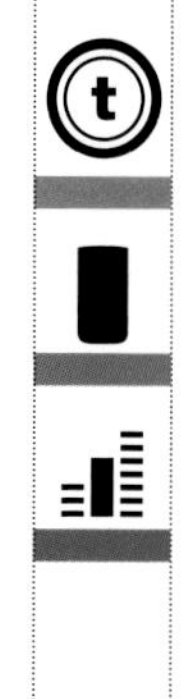

Ice

- **3 ounces blanco tequila**
- **2 ounces fresh grapefruit juice**
- **½ ounce fresh lime juice**
- **½ ounce Rosemary Syrup (below)**
- **1 ounce chilled club soda**

Fill a cocktail shaker with ice. Add the tequila, grapefruit juice, lime juice and Rosemary Syrup and shake well. Strain into an ice-filled highball glass and stir in the club soda.

rosemary syrup

In a small saucepan, bring 6 ounces Simple Syrup (p. 20) to a boil. Remove from the heat and add 2 rosemary sprigs. Let cool, then cover and refrigerate overnight. Strain the syrup into a jar, cover and refrigerate for up to 3 weeks. Makes 6 ounces.

latin trifecta

Ice
1 ounce blanco tequila
1 ounce Cynar (bitter artichoke liqueur)
½ ounce dry sherry
3 dashes of orange bitters
1 orange twist, flamed (p. 16), for garnish

Fill a pint glass with ice. Add the tequila, Cynar, sherry and orange bitters and stir well. Strain into a chilled coupe and garnish with the flamed orange twist.

jupiter olympus

With this vermouth-based drink, Boudreau pays tribute to legendary 19th-century author and bartender Jerry Thomas. Thomas purportedly had a fondness for fortified wines, including vermouth.

Ice
2 ounces dry vermouth
1 ounce sweet vermouth
Dash of maraschino liqueur
1 lemon twist, for garnish

Fill a pint glass with ice. Add both vermouths and the maraschino liqueur and stir well. Strain into a chilled coupe and garnish with the lemon twist.

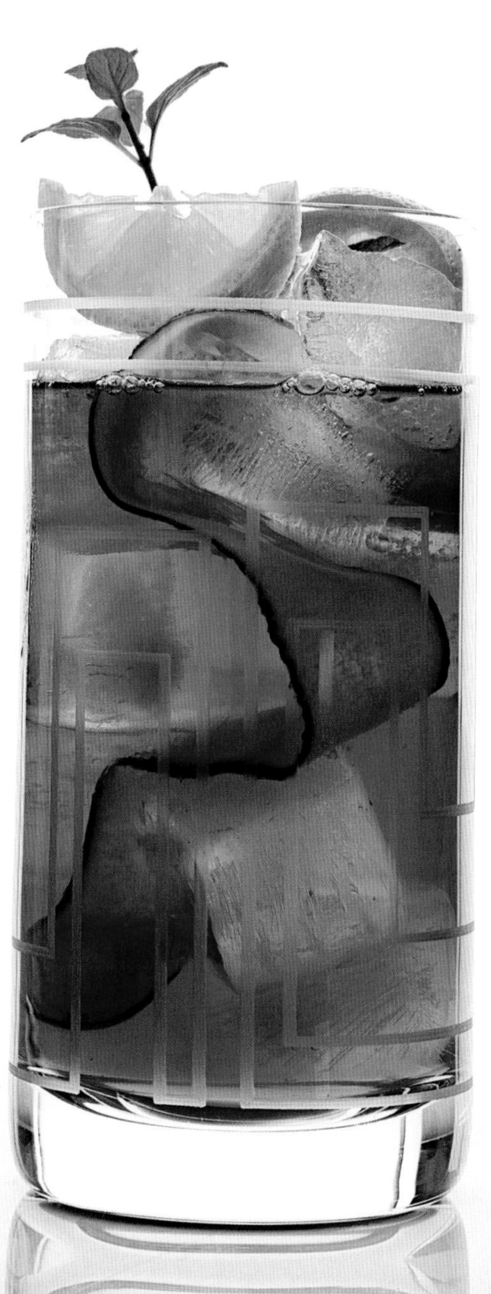

Pimm's Iced Tea

"Dedalo" highball by Versace for Rosenthal.

pimm's iced tea

Pimm's No. 1, a gin-based aperitif invented by London bar owner James Pimm in 1823, is the quintessential English summer-afternoon drink (and the traditional drink of Wimbledon). Here, Boudreau combines it with tea, another beloved British beverage.

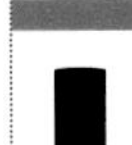

Ice
3 ounces Pimm's No. 1
6 ounces chilled brewed orange pekoe tea
¼ ounce agave nectar
¼ ounce fresh lemon juice
Citrus wedges, mint sprigs and/or cucumber ribbons, for garnish

Fill a highball glass with ice. Add the Pimm's, tea, agave nectar and lemon juice and stir well. Garnish the drink lavishly.

helene bracer

The inspiration behind this lively cocktail is Picon Bière, a mixture of pilsner and Amer Picon (an orange-flavored bitter) that's poured in French cafés. Boudreau replaces the traditional French bitter with spicy Italian Montenegro amaro.

Ice
1½ ounces Montenegro amaro
6 ounces chilled lager
1 orange twist, for garnish

Fill a collins glass with ice. Add the amaro and lager and stir gently. Garnish with the orange twist.

Cilantro Cooler

"Raki" glasses from the "Liquids" collection by Gaia & Gino.

cilantro cooler

According to Boudreau, a good aperitif often hints at the meal that will follow. This light, summery cilantro-spiked drink—which Boudreau likes to mix with a eucalyptus-infused simple syrup—would be a great lead-up to Mexican food.

- ½ cup chopped cucumber
- 5 cilantro leaves, plus 1 flowering cilantro sprig for garnish (optional)
- Ice
- 2 ounces vodka
- ¾ ounce fresh lime juice
- ¾ ounce Simple Syrup (p. 20)
- 1 ounce chilled club soda

In a cocktail shaker, muddle the cucumber and cilantro leaves. Add ice and the vodka, lime juice and Simple Syrup and shake well. Double strain (p. 17) into an ice-filled collins glass, stir in the club soda and garnish.

royal woodhouse

The Royal Woodhouse is Boudreau's adaptation of the Bellini (Prosecco and peach nectar). It's also a nod to 18th-century English merchant and entrepreneur John Woodhouse, who is credited with discovering Marsala wine.

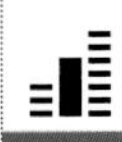

- ¼ fresh peach
- Ice
- 2 ounces dry Marsala
- Dash of peach bitters
- 3 ounces chilled Champagne

In a cocktail shaker, muddle the peach. Add ice and the Marsala and bitters and shake well. Strain into a chilled flute and top with the Champagne.

Bitter Peach

"Tyrol" glasses by Riedel.

sicilian vesper

Vesper refers to the period when late afternoon segues into early evening, the typical time for an aperitif. Marsala wine, which comes from Sicily, gives the drink a dry, nutty quality.

Ice
2 ounces dry Marsala
½ ounce Poire Williams
¼ ounce cream sherry
Dash of Angostura bitters

Fill a pint glass with ice. Add all of the remaining ingredients and stir well, then strain into a chilled coupe.

bitter peach

While playing with leftover ingredients one night, Boudreau combined grappa and peach puree. The mixture was sweet, so he added Aperol, a bitter orange liqueur, then Champagne, resulting in this well-balanced cocktail.

Ice
1½ ounces grappa
½ ounce Aperol
½ ounce peach puree or nectar
2 ounces chilled Champagne
1 peach slice, for garnish (optional)

Fill a cocktail shaker with ice. Add the grappa, Aperol and peach puree and shake well. Strain into a chilled coupe, top with the Champagne and garnish with the peach slice.

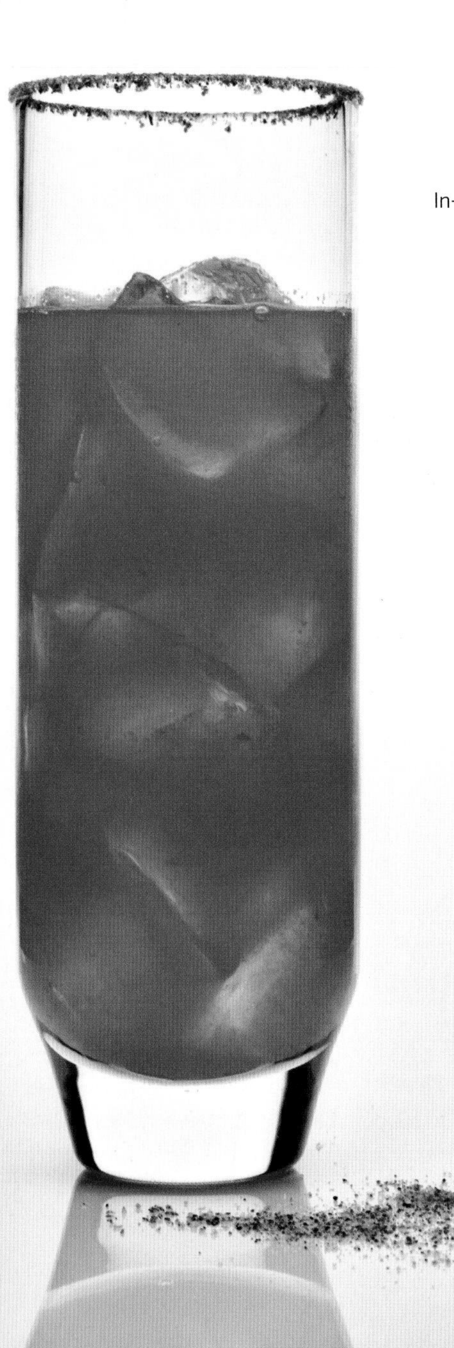

In-Sandíary, p. 51

LATIN DRINKS

recipes by joaquin simo

MEET THE MIXOLOGIST

joaquin simo

Driven by his passion for the perfect daiquiri, Ecuadorean-born Joaquin Simo meticulously tested all of the recipes for this book by day while slinging cocktails (both Latin and otherwise) at the exclusive Manhattan bar Death & Co. by night. (He was a founding bartender there.) Simo is obsessed with food-and-cocktail pairings; his favorite is his Solera Sidecar (p. 62) with fried sweetbreads.

michelada

This zingy Mexican drink is often made with pilsner (a light, hoppy beer), but Simo prefers to use a dark, malty brew instead.

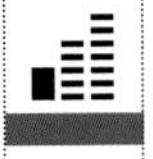

- 1 lime wedge and kosher salt
- Ice
- 1 bottle (12 ounces) chilled dark Mexican beer, such as Negra Modelo
- ¾ ounce fresh lime juice
- ¼ ounce fresh orange juice
- 2 or 3 dashes of chipotle pepper sauce
- 2 dashes of Maggi Seasoning Sauce or Worcestershire sauce

Moisten half of the outer rim of a pint glass with the lime wedge and coat lightly with salt. Fill the glass with ice. Add the beer, lime juice, orange juice, chipotle sauce and Maggi Seasoning and stir.

in-sandíary

This cocktail's name is a play on both the Spanish word for watermelon, sandía, *and "incendiary," referring to the peppery tequila and the spicy ancho chile rim.*

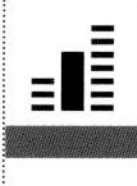

1 lime wedge and chile salt (a mixture of 1 teaspoon each of kosher salt, sugar and ancho chile powder)
Ice
2 ounces blanco tequila
2 ounces watermelon juice
½ ounce fresh lime juice
¼ ounce Simple Syrup (p. 20)

Moisten the outer rim of a highball glass with the lime wedge and coat lightly with chile salt. Fill a cocktail shaker with ice. Add all of the remaining ingredients and shake well. Fill the highball glass with ice and strain the drink into the glass.

yerba mora

"The thing about good traditional Mexican food," says Simo, "is that you can never tell exactly what's in it. It's the same with cocktails."

5 blackberries, plus 3 blackberries skewered on a pick for garnish
Ice
2 ounces blanco tequila
½ ounce green Chartreuse
Dash of absinthe
1 ounce fresh lime juice
1 ounce Honey Syrup (p. 54)
5 cilantro leaves

In a cocktail shaker, muddle the 5 blackberries. Add ice and all of the remaining ingredients except the skewered blackberries and shake well. Strain into an ice-filled highball glass and garnish with the skewered blackberries.

Flor de Jalisco

"Patrician" Champagne cup by Lobmeyr from Neue Galerie.

flor de jalisco

The margarita-like Flor de Jalisco is a nod to Simo's friend Sam Kershaw, a Scottish bartender who's obsessed with using jams and other fruit preserves as cocktail ingredients.

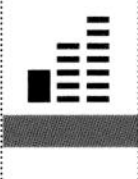

Ice
- **2 ounces blanco tequila**
- **¾ ounce fresh lemon juice**
- **½ ounce agave nectar**
- **1 teaspoon orange marmalade**
- **1 orange twist, for garnish**

Fill a cocktail shaker with ice. Add all of the remaining ingredients except the twist and shake well. Strain into a chilled coupe and garnish with the orange twist.

la bomba daiquiri

This daiquiri defies the idea that fruity drinks always have to be supersweet by combining tangy raspberries and tart pomegranate molasses.

- **5 raspberries**

Ice
- **2 ounces white rum**
- **¾ ounce fresh lime juice**
- **½ ounce Simple Syrup (p. 20)**
- **1 teaspoon pomegranate molasses**

In a cocktail shaker, muddle the raspberries. Add ice and all of the remaining ingredients and shake well. Double strain (p. 17) into a chilled coupe.

honeysuckle with absinthe

This is an updated version of the little-known classic cocktail Honeysuckle from David Embury's 1948 The Fine Art of Mixing Drinks.

Ice
2 ounces white rum
1 or 2 dashes of absinthe
¾ ounce Honey Syrup (below)
¾ ounce fresh lime juice

Fill a cocktail shaker with ice. Add all of the remaining ingredients and shake well. Strain the drink into a chilled coupe.

honey syrup

In a jar, combine 1 cup honey with 1 cup hot water. Close tightly and shake the mixture well. Refrigerate the Honey Syrup for up to 1 month. Makes about 12 ounces.

punky monkey

Simo named this tiki-style cocktail after his fiancée, Rhea, whom he calls Monkey ("Punky when she's being a smarty-pants," he says). The powerful cardamom flavor is a nod to her love of Indian spices.

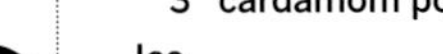

- 3 cardamom pods
- Ice
- 1 ounce aged rum
- 1 ounce bourbon, preferably overproof
- ½ ounce agave nectar
- ½ ounce pineapple juice
- ½ ounce fresh lemon juice
- Dash of Angostura bitters
- Dash of Peychaud's bitters
- 1 cardamom shoot, for garnish (optional)

In a cocktail shaker, lightly muddle the cardamom pods. Add ice and all of the remaining ingredients except the cardamom shoot and shake well. Strain into a chilled coupe and garnish.

latin quarter

This rum-based spin on the quintessential New Orleans cocktail, the rye- or brandy-based Sazerac, is named for the Big Easy neighborhood where the drink was supposedly created.

- ¼ ounce absinthe
- Ice
- 2 ounces aged rum
- 1 teaspoon Rich Simple Syrup (p. 20)
- Dash of Angostura bitters
- 3 dashes of Peychaud's bitters
- Dash of Bittermens Xocolatl mole bitters (optional)
- 1 lemon twist

Rinse a chilled rocks glass with the absinthe, then pour it out. Fill a pint glass with ice. Add all of the remaining ingredients except the twist and stir well. Strain into the rocks glass. Pinch the twist over the drink, rub it around the rim and discard.

Strawberry-Lemon Mojito

"Colombina" flutes by Alessi.

strawberry-lemon mojito

"This is a great drink when you're in the mood for something fruity," says Simo. Use a molasses-based rum (like white Brugal) for a smoother drink, or a sugarcane-based rum (such as white Barbancourt) for a drier cocktail.

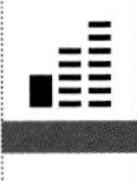

- 2 lemon wedges
- 6 to 8 mint leaves, plus 1 mint sprig for garnish (optional)
- 1 strawberry, plus 1 strawberry half for garnish
- Ice cubes, plus crushed ice
- 2 ounces aged rum
- ¾ ounce fresh lemon juice
- ½ ounce store-bought sugarcane syrup or agave nectar

In a cocktail shaker, muddle the lemon with the mint leaves and whole strawberry. Add ice cubes and the rum, lemon juice and syrup; shake well. Strain into a crushed ice–filled highball glass; garnish with the berry half and mint sprig.

new england daiquiri

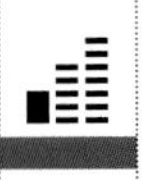

- Ice
- 1 ounce dark rum
- 1 ounce aged rum, preferably Jamaican
- ½ ounce pure maple syrup
- ½ ounce fresh lemon juice

Fill a cocktail shaker with ice. Add the dark rum, aged rum, pure maple syrup and lemon juice and shake well. Strain into a chilled coupe.

improved rum cocktail

This drink was inspired by cocktail historian David Wondrich's 2007 book Imbibe!, *a salute to pioneering 19th-century bartender Jerry Thomas that includes recipes for "Plain," "Fancy," "Improved" and "Evolved" drinks.*

Ice
2 ounces aged rum
½ teaspoon maraschino liqueur
Dash of absinthe
½ teaspoon Rich Simple Syrup (p. 20)
Dash of Angostura bitters
Dash of Peychaud's bitters
1 lemon twist, for garnish

Fill a pint glass with ice. Add the aged rum, maraschino liqueur, absinthe, Rich Simple Syrup, Angostura bitters and Peychaud's bitters and stir well. Strain the drink into an ice-filled rocks glass and garnish with the lemon twist.

autumn daiquiri

Originally from Cuba, the daiquiri is usually a warm-weather cocktail. This version's spiced flavors are perfect for cooler months. Add any leftover Cinnamon Syrup to mulled wine or punch, or pour it over vanilla ice cream with a few dashes of Angostura bitters.

Ice
2 ounces aged or spiced rum
¾ ounce fresh lime juice
½ ounce pineapple juice
¼ ounce Rich Simple Syrup (p. 20)
¼ ounce Cinnamon Syrup (below)
Dash of Angostura bitters

Fill a cocktail shaker with ice. Add all of the remaining ingredients and shake well. Strain the drink into a chilled coupe.

cinnamon syrup

In a small saucepan, bring 1 cup water to a boil with 1 cup sugar and 6 medium cinnamon sticks broken into pieces. Simmer over moderate heat for 2 minutes, stirring to dissolve the sugar. Let cool, cover and let stand for 4 hours. Strain the syrup into a jar, cover and refrigerate for up to 1 month. Makes about 12 ounces.

Caribbean Shrub

"Cura" glasses by Nouvel Studio.

caribbean shrub

Shrubs were originally made in Colonial America. They typically combined rum and a gastrique, a syrup made with vinegar, sugar and, often, seasonal fruits such as strawberries.

2 ice cubes, plus crushed ice
1 ounce dark rum
1 ounce white rhum agricole
¾ ounce Strawberry-Balsamic Gastrique (below)
1 small strawberry, for garnish

Put the ice cubes in a cocktail shaker. Add both rums and the gastrique and shake well. Strain the drink into a crushed ice–filled highball glass and garnish with the strawberry.

strawberry-balsamic gastrique

In a medium saucepan, stir 1⅓ cups superfine sugar into 1⅓ cups hot water until dissolved. Add 2 cups halved hulled strawberries and simmer over low heat for 30 minutes. Add 1 cup balsamic vinegar, increase the heat and bring to a boil. Reduce the heat to low and simmer until thickened, about 30 minutes. Let the gastrique cool, then strain into a jar, cover and refrigerate for up to 3 weeks. Makes about 8 ounces.

solera sidecar

Simo invented this take on the sidecar for a cocktail-pairing dinner hosted by the underground supper club New York Bite Club. He matched the nutty drink with fried sweetbreads.

Ice
1½ ounces brandy, preferably Spanish
¾ ounce manzanilla sherry
½ ounce Licor 43 (citrus-and-vanilla-flavored liqueur)
¾ ounce fresh lemon juice

Fill a cocktail shaker with ice. Add all of the remaining ingredients and shake well. Strain into a chilled coupe.

mucho picchu

This South American riff on the classic French 75 replaces gin with pisco (a South American brandy) and lemon juice with grapefruit juice.

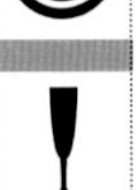

Ice
1½ ounces pisco
1 teaspoon maraschino liqueur
½ ounce fresh grapefruit juice
½ ounce Simple Syrup (p. 20)
2 ounces chilled Champagne
1 grapefruit twist

Fill a cocktail shaker with ice. Add all of the remaining ingredients except the Champagne and the twist and shake well. Strain into a flute and top with the Champagne. Pinch the twist over the drink, rub it around the rim and discard.

little birdy

The name of this drink's primary ingredient, pisco, is said to be derived from the word "bird" in Quechua, a native South American language.

Ice
2 ounces Strawberry-Pineapple Pisco (below)
½ ounce St-Germain elderflower liqueur
¾ ounce fresh grapefruit juice
½ ounce fresh lemon juice
1 teaspoon Simple Syrup (p. 20)

Fill a cocktail shaker with ice. Add all of the remaining ingredients and shake well. Strain the drink into a chilled coupe.

LATIN DRINKS

strawberry-pineapple pisco

In a large jar, combine 5 cups chopped fresh pineapple and 5 cups sliced hulled strawberries with 1 bottle (750 ml) pisco. Cover and refrigerate for 5 days. Strain into the pisco bottle or another large jar, cover and refrigerate for up to 1 month. Makes about 25 ounces.

Pear of Desire, p. 67

"Ming Yiu" glass by Karim Rashid for Gaia & Gino.

SEASONAL DRINKS

recipes by todd thrasher

MEET THE MIXOLOGIST

todd thrasher

Sommelier at Restaurant Eve, mixologist at speakeasy PX and creator of egg creams at the Majestic (all in Alexandria, Virginia), Todd Thrasher was inspired to experiment with unlikely ingredients like pickled foams and peach "airs" by chefs he's worked with (like José Andrés). Despite his avant-garde tendencies, he's an ingredient purist. Restaurant Eve never serves produce out of season, and neither does Thrasher.

big O

During the cold months—prime season for citrus fruits—Thrasher sometimes makes this drink using up to five different varieties of oranges.

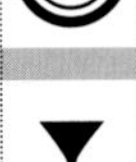

Ice
1 ounce orange vodka, preferably Stolichnaya Ohranj
½ ounce Cointreau or other triple sec
2 ounces blood orange juice
1 ounce Simple Syrup (p. 20)
Large dash of orange bitters
Large dash of Angostura bitters

Fill a cocktail shaker with ice. Add all of the remaining ingredients and shake well. Strain the drink into a chilled martini glass.

pear of desire

When naming this pear-flavored cocktail, Thrasher turned to a French quote on Restaurant Eve's dining room wall. It roughly translates as: "The savage man eats out of necessity; the civilized man eats out of desire."

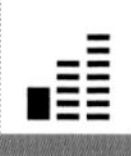

Ice
- **¾ ounce citrus vodka**
- **¾ ounce Licor 43 (citrus-and-vanilla-flavored liqueur)**
- **2 ounces pear juice or nectar**
- **½ ounce cream soda**
- **1 ounce chilled ginger ale**

1 or 2 pear slices, for garnish (optional)

Fill a pint glass with ice. Add all of the remaining ingredients except the ginger ale and pear slices and stir well. Strain into a chilled coupe, top with the ginger ale and garnish with the pear slices.

spiced melon

- **10 mint leaves**
- **3 pink peppercorns**
- **¾ teaspoon Champagne vinegar**

Ice
- **2 ounces Lillet blanc**
- **1 ounce citrus vodka**
- **½ ounce Simple Syrup (p. 20)**
- **3 ounces watermelon juice**

In a cocktail shaker, muddle the mint and peppercorns with the vinegar. Add ice and the Lillet, vodka and Simple Syrup and shake well. Stir in the watermelon juice and double strain (p. 17) into a chilled coupe.

Peach Donkey

"Kikatsu" highball glass from Eastern Accent.

peach donkey

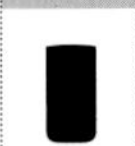

1 ounce vodka
½ ounce ginger liqueur
3 ounces peach puree or nectar
Crushed ice
1 ounce chilled ginger beer
Peach slices, for garnish (optional)

In a highball glass, combine the vodka, ginger liqueur and peach puree; stir. Add crushed ice and stir again. Top with the ginger beer and swizzle by spinning a swizzle stick or bar spoon between your hands. Garnish with peach slices.

mary is getting fresh

Thrasher's aversion to using canned ingredients in his cocktails prompted this light and fresh variation on the Bloody Mary.

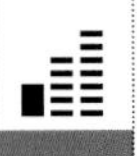

1 small plum tomato
1 lemon wedge
1 lime wedge
1 teaspoon diced red onion
1 teaspoon diced seeded jalapeño
1 teaspoon prepared horseradish
4 cilantro sprigs
Dash of Worcestershire sauce
Pinch each of salt and freshly ground pepper
Ice
2 ounces vodka

In a cocktail shaker, muddle all of the ingredients except ice and the vodka. Add ice and the vodka and shake well. Strain into an ice-filled highball glass.

Sweet Basil

"Dagmar" glass by Theresienthal.

sweet basil

An abundance of basil growing behind Restaurant Eve inspired this drink. Thrasher created six basil cocktails, rotating them on the menu at PX. This one had the most fanatical following.

10 basil leaves, plus 1 basil leaf for garnish
Ice
3 ounces Lillet blanc
½ ounce gin
1 ounce Simple Syrup (p. 20)

In a cocktail shaker, lightly muddle the 10 basil leaves. Add ice and the Lillet, gin and Simple Syrup and shake well. Double strain (p. 17) into a chilled coupe and garnish with the remaining basil leaf.

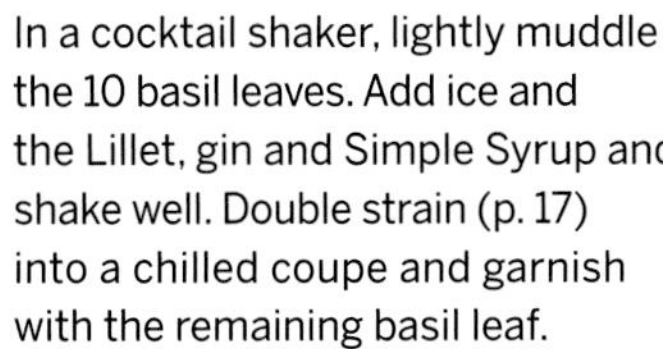

boris karloff

This drink's moniker refers to one of the original actors in the play Arsenic and Old Lace, *in which two sisters murder a series of men with poisoned elderberry wine.*

¾ ounce gin
¾ ounce St-Germain elderflower liqueur
1 ounce fresh lime juice
1 tablespoon confectioners' sugar
1 large egg white
Ice
1 ounce chilled club soda
Pinch each of finely grated lime zest and freshly ground pepper, for garnish

In a cocktail shaker, combine the gin, elderflower liqueur, lime juice, sugar and egg white. Shake well. Add ice and shake again. Strain into an ice-filled collins glass, stir in the club soda and garnish with the lime zest and pepper.

josef the spy

The strawberry-rhubarb mixture in this cocktail pays homage to Todd Thrasher's grandmother, Alice Thrasher, who taught him how to pick the best rhubarb for her famous strawberry-rhubarb pie.

Ice
1 ounce tequila
½ ounce Cointreau or other triple sec
3 ounces Strawberry-Rhubarb Syrup (below)
3 drops of balsamic vinegar
1 ounce chilled Sprite

Fill a cocktail shaker with ice. Add all of the remaining ingredients except the Sprite and shake well. Strain the drink into an ice-filled highball glass and stir in the Sprite.

strawberry-rhubarb syrup

Trim and coarsely chop 4 stalks of rhubarb, then puree in a blender with 2½ ounces (½ cup) hulled strawberries and 1 cup Simple Syrup (p. 20) until smooth. Strain the syrup into a jar, cover and refrigerate for up to 4 days. Makes about 14 ounces.

the loser

At Tales of the Cocktail 2006, a cocktail festival held in New Orleans, Thrasher entered the Bar Chef competition with this drink; although it's terrific, it lost. The drink now resides on the menu at PX.

Ice
1 ounce pisco
½ ounce Velvet Falernum (clove-spiced liqueur)
3 ounces pineapple juice
1 ounce fresh lemon juice
½ ounce Black Pepper Syrup (below)
1 ounce chilled club soda
Pinch of freshly ground pepper, for garnish

Fill a cocktail shaker with ice. Add all of the remaining ingredients except the soda and ground pepper; shake well. Strain into an ice-filled highball glass. Stir in the soda; garnish with the pepper.

black pepper syrup

In a small saucepan, bring 1 cup water to a boil. Add ½ cup sugar and stir over moderately high heat until dissolved. Add ¼ cup coarsely cracked black peppercorns and let stand off the heat for 20 minutes. Strain the syrup into a jar, cover and refrigerate for up to 3 weeks. Makes about 8 ounces.

Carrot Colada

"Arctic" glass by Nasonmoretti.

carrot colada

A Thai curry of carrots with coconut milk gave Thrasher the idea for this drink.

Ice
1 ounce white rum
1 ounce coconut rum
1½ ounces coconut water
1 ounce carrot juice
1 ounce clementine or orange juice
1 or 2 halved baby carrots, for garnish (optional)

Fill a cocktail shaker with ice. Add all of the remaining ingredients except the garnish and shake well. Strain the drink into an ice-filled highball glass and garnish with the halved baby carrots.

grog

In the 18th century, the British navy gave its men a water-and-rum mixture called grog. Thrasher serves his Grog in glass-bottomed mugs because, he says, sailors and pirates drank it that way so they could always watch out for their enemies.

Ice
1½ ounces spiced rum, preferably Captain Morgan
3 ounces chilled brewed lemon verbena tea (verveine)
1 tablespoon confectioners' sugar
2 teaspoons fresh orange juice
2 teaspoons fresh lemon juice
2 teaspoons fresh lime juice
Dash of lemon bitters
1 lemon wedge, for garnish

Fill a cocktail shaker with ice. Add all of the remaining ingredients except the lemon wedge and shake well. Strain into an ice-filled highball glass and garnish with the lemon wedge.

mt. kenny fizz

- ½ ounce aged rum, preferably Mount Gay
- ½ ounce Cognac
- ½ ounce Velvet Falernum (clove-spiced liqueur)
- 3 ounces pineapple juice
- ½ teaspoon light brown sugar, plus a pinch for garnish
- Pinch of freshly grated nutmeg, plus a pinch for garnish
- 1 large egg white
- Ice

In a cocktail shaker, combine all of the ingredients except the garnishes and ice and shake well. Add ice and shake again. Strain into a chilled coupe and garnish.

jefferson's crimson

Thomas Jefferson is credited as being one of the first people to grow pomegranates in the United States, having planted a crop of the fruit trees at Monticello in 1769.

- 2 tablespoons pomegranate molasses and 2 tablespoons sugar
- Ice
- ¾ ounce Southern Comfort
- ¾ ounce bourbon, preferably Maker's Mark
- 3 ounces pomegranate juice
- ½ ounce pomegranate molasses
- ½ ounce fresh lemon juice

Moisten the outer rim of a rocks glass with the 2 tablespoons of pomegranate molasses and coat lightly with the sugar. Fill a cocktail shaker with ice. Add all of the remaining ingredients and shake well. Fill the rocks glass with ice and strain the drink into the glass.

sherlock holmes

This smoky cocktail is a nod to Sir Arthur Conan Doyle's fictitious British detective, whose favorite tea was purportedly Lapsang souchong.

Ice
1½ ounces single-malt Scotch, preferably Laphroaig
2 ounces chilled brewed Lapsang souchong tea
1 ounce Honey Syrup (p. 54)
¾ ounce fresh lemon juice

Fill a cocktail shaker with ice. Add all of the remaining ingredients and stir well. Double strain (p. 17) into a chilled coupe.

irish flip

The name "flip" traditionally refers to cocktails made with eggs. These drinks fell out of fashion decades ago, but Thrasher is working to bring them back. His rich, eggnog-like Irish Flip is on PX's winter menu.

1½ ounces Irish whiskey
1 large egg
1 tablespoon confectioners' sugar
1 ounce half-and-half
Ice
Pinch of freshly grated nutmeg, for garnish

In a cocktail shaker, combine all of the ingredients except ice and the nutmeg and shake well. Add ice and shake again. Strain into a chilled coupe and garnish with the grated nutmeg.

Peppermint Paddy

peppermint paddy

Thrasher loves reproducing the flavors of classic candies in cocktails. The Peppermint Paddy is his take on his wife Maria's favorite guilty pleasure.

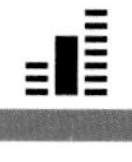

1 ounce brandy
1 ounce white crème de menthe
½ ounce dark rum
4 ounces white hot chocolate
Chocolate-flavored whipped cream and crushed Peppermint Altoids, for garnish (optional)

Combine the brandy, white crème de menthe, dark rum and hot chocolate in a heatproof mug and stir. Top with the chocolate whipped cream and crushed Altoids.

cider car

Appley Calvados, hot apple cider and cinnamon sugar make this spin on the sidecar a great fall drink.

1 lime wedge and cinnamon sugar (a mixture of 2 tablespoons each of sugar and ground cinnamon)
1½ ounces Calvados, preferably Busnel
½ ounce Cointreau or other triple sec
5 ounces hot apple cider

Moisten the outer rim of a heatproof mug with the lime wedge and coat lightly with the cinnamon sugar. Add the Calvados, Cointreau and hot apple cider and stir well.

Spice & Ice, p. 84

"Verona" glass by Nouvel Studio.

FROZEN DRINKS

recipes by adam seger

MEET THE MIXOLOGIST

adam seger

Adam Seger's penchant for blender drinks started early: He loved mixing cinnamon-and-vanilla-spiked banana smoothies as a kid. At Nacional 27 in Chicago, he creates terrific frozen drinks and more using local produce and his own house-made liqueurs, mixers and bitters. Seger is now working on a book called *WHET: Drink Like You Eat* and developing a line of high-end mixers for the Perfect Purée of Napa Valley.

ginger-hibiscus freeze

For Seger, frozen drinks recall exotic vacations. He plays up that idea here by combining the tropical flavors of ginger, hibiscus flower and lime.

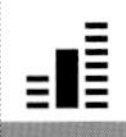

MAKES 6 DRINKS

- **1 lime wedge and ginger sugar (a mixture of 3 tablespoons superfine sugar, 2 tablespoons ground ginger and 1 tablespoon ground cardamom)**
- **12 ounces ginger liqueur**
- **5 ounces fresh lime juice**
- **2 tablespoons dried hibiscus flowers**
- **4 cups ice**

Moisten half of the outer rim of 6 chilled white wine glasses with the lime wedge and coat lightly with the ginger sugar. In a blender, combine all of the remaining ingredients and blend until smooth. Pour into the wineglasses.

passion colada

This drink combines passion fruit with two classic cocktails: the mojito (rum, mint and lime) and the piña colada (rum, coconut and pineapple).

MAKES 6 DRINKS

- 6 ounces dark rum
- 6 ounces passion fruit puree or nectar
- 5 ounces pineapple juice
- 4 ounces fresh lime juice
- 2½ ounces cream of coconut from a well-shaken can
- 5 cups ice
- 6 pineapple wedges and 6 mint sprigs, for garnish

In a blender, combine all of the ingredients except the garnishes and blend until smooth. Pour into chilled white wine glasses and garnish.

watermelon-honey-citrus refresher

One great thing about blender drinks: The machine does all the work. Seger prefers Vita-Mix blenders, which create especially smooth purees.

MAKES 6 DRINKS

- 8 ounces chilled vodka or pisco
- 3 cups coarsely chopped seedless watermelon
- 1 cup honey
- 4 ounces fresh lemon juice
- Finely grated zest of 2 lemons
- 2 ounces fresh red grapefruit juice
- 4 cups ice
- 6 watermelon wedges, for garnish

In a blender, combine all of the ingredients except the watermelon wedges and blend until smooth. Pour into chilled highball glasses and garnish with the watermelon wedges.

spice & ice

At Nacional 27, Seger coats the rim of the Spice & Ice glass with lime and a seven-spice blend that includes ground cinnamon, ginger, fennel seeds, clove, star anise, cardamom pods, Sichuan peppercorns and sugar.

MAKES 4 DRINKS

6 ounces blanco tequila
5 ounces mango puree or nectar
5 ounces fresh lime juice
Finely grated zest of 1 lime
4 ounces Ginger-Habanero Syrup (below)
4 cups ice
4 lime wheels, for garnish

In a blender, combine all of the ingredients except the lime wheels and blend until smooth. Pour into chilled martini glasses and garnish with the lime wheels.

ginger-habanero syrup

In a small saucepan, combine 1 cup water, 1 cup sugar, 2 ounces sliced fresh ginger and 1 halved seeded habanero. Bring to a boil over moderately high heat, stirring to dissolve the sugar, about 3 minutes. Let cool completely, then discard the habanero. Strain the syrup into a jar, cover and refrigerate for up to 3 weeks. Makes about 12 ounces.

bloody margarita

Seger prefers tequila to vodka for his Bloody Marys (and his Bloody Margaritas) because it's more acidic and herbal. At Nacional 27, he makes Bloody Mary mix with ketchup, using a recipe adapted from his hometown's Baton Rouge Country Club.

MAKES 4 DRINKS

- 1 lime wedge and spiced salt (a mixture of 2 tablespoons each of kosher salt and freshly ground pepper, 1 tablespoon pure chile powder and 1 teaspoon ground celery seeds)
- 8 ounces reposado tequila
- 4 ounces fresh orange juice
- 2½ ounces fresh lime juice
- 1 cup prepared Bloody Mary mix, frozen
- 2 cups ice
- 4 pickled jalapeños, for garnish

Moisten half of the outer rim of 4 chilled rocks glasses with the lime wedge and coat lightly with the spiced salt. In a blender, combine the tequila, orange juice, lime juice, Bloody Mary mix and ice and blend until smooth. Pour into the rocks glasses and garnish with the pickled jalapeños.

Aphrodisiac Margarita

"Mitos" glass by Arik Levy for Květná from Ameico.

aphrodisiac margarita

Seger claims that the margarita is the cocktail world's aphrodisiac. This version combines passion fruit and pomegranate, commonly associated with Aphrodite, the goddess of love.

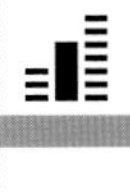

MAKES 6 DRINKS

- 1 lime wedge and peppery salt (a mixture of 2 tablespoons each of freshly ground pepper and kosher salt)
- 8 ounces blanco tequila
- 5 ounces passion fruit puree or nectar
- 4 ounces fresh lime juice
- 2½ ounces pomegranate juice
- 2 ounces fresh blood orange juice
- 2 ounces Simple Syrup (p. 20)
- 4 cups ice

Moisten half of the outer rim of 6 chilled coupes or martini glasses with the lime wedge and coat lightly with the peppery salt. In a blender, combine the tequila, passion fruit puree, lime juice, pomegranate juice, blood orange juice, Simple Syrup and ice and blend until smooth. Pour the margarita into the glasses.

Cucumber-
Honeydew Freeze

"Newport" goblet
by Theresienthal.

cucumber-honeydew freeze

Fruit flavors generally mix well if they're from the same botanical family. This cool and light summer cocktail works because cucumber and melon both belong to the Cucurbitaceae family.

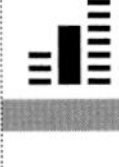

MAKES 6 DRINKS

- **1 lime wedge and sweet fennel salt (a mixture of 2 tablespoons each of kosher salt, sugar and ground fennel seeds)**
- **8 ounces gin**
- **2 cups chilled chopped peeled cucumber**
- **2 cups chilled chopped honeydew melon**
- **6 ounces fresh lemon juice**
- **1 cup honey**
- **5 cups ice**

Cucumber wheels and honeydew melon balls, for garnish

Moisten half of the outer rim of 6 chilled white wine glasses with the lime wedge and coat lightly with the sweet fennel salt. In a blender, combine all of the remaining ingredients except the garnishes and blend until smooth. Pour the drink into the glasses. Garnish the drinks with the cucumber wheels and honeydew melon balls.

Blueberry-Maple Caiprissimo
"BAR" tumbler from Lekker.

blueberry-maple caiprissimo

A blueberry-rosemary flan that Seger's friend Ann Giles created for the Chicago restaurant DeLaCosta led to this cocktail's unlikely mix of flavors.

MAKES 4 DRINKS

- **6 ounces bourbon or Cognac**
- **6 ounces blueberries, plus 4 blueberries, each skewered on a rosemary sprig, for garnish (optional)**
- **6 ounces Maple-Rosemary Syrup (below)**
- **4 ounces fresh lemon juice**
- **3 cups ice**

In a blender, combine all of the ingredients except the skewered blueberries and blend until smooth. Pour the drinks into chilled rocks glasses and garnish.

maple-rosemary syrup

In a microwave-safe bowl, combine 4 rosemary sprigs with 6 ounces pure maple syrup. Microwave on high power until hot, about 30 seconds. Let the syrup cool, then discard the rosemary sprigs. Transfer the syrup to a jar, cover and refrigerate for up to 3 weeks. Makes about 6 ounces.

frozen sangria

Frozen drinks are perfect for entertaining, says Seger: "You just rev up a blender with some fresh fruit and you have a party."

MAKES 4 DRINKS

- 16 ounces fruity red wine
- 4 ounces peach schnapps
- 4 ounces Grand Marnier
- 8 ounces fresh orange juice
- Finely grated zest of 2 oranges
- ½ teaspoon ground cinnamon
- Pinch of ground cloves
- ¼ apple, coarsely chopped
- 4 cups ice
- 4 apple wedges and 4 orange wheels, for garnish

In a blender, combine all of the ingredients except the garnishes and blend until smooth. Pour into red wine glasses and garnish.

strawberry-basil-balsamic daiquiri

This pleasantly sweet-tangy drink was inspired by the classic Italian pairing of strawberries and balsamic vinegar.

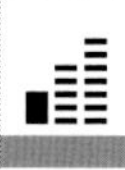

MAKES 4 DRINKS

- 8 ounces dark rum
- 1 cup halved hulled fresh strawberries, plus 4 whole strawberries for garnish
- ¼ cup light brown sugar
- ¼ cup loosely packed basil leaves
- 1 tablespoon aged balsamic vinegar
- ½ pint strawberry ice cream
- 2 cups ice

In a blender, combine all of the ingredients except the whole strawberries and blend until smooth. Pour into chilled red wine glasses and garnish with the strawberries.

mocha-spice freeze

Seger believes that a great rim on a cocktail takes the integral flavor components of a drink (in this case, cocoa, coffee and sugar) and combines them with complementary flavors (like the allspice here).

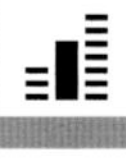

MAKES 4 DRINKS

- **1 orange wedge and mocha sugar (a mixture of 2 tablespoons each of sugar, ground allspice, instant coffee and cocoa powder)**
- **8 ounces spiced rum**
- **¼ cup unsweetened cocoa powder**
- **¼ cup instant coffee**
- **¼ cup light brown sugar**
- **1 pint vanilla ice cream**
- **2 cups ice**

Moisten the outer rim of 4 chilled martini glasses with the orange; coat lightly with the mocha sugar. In a blender, combine all of the remaining ingredients and blend until smooth. Pour into the glasses.

frozen bananas foster

For Seger, this drink evokes memories of the Bananas Foster at Brennan's Restaurant in New Orleans. He makes sure a version of the dessert is on the menu wherever he works.

MAKES 6 DRINKS

- **10 ounces bourbon**
- **4 bananas**
- **4 ounces fresh orange juice**
- **1 cup prepared caramel sauce**
- **1 pint vanilla ice cream**
- **3 cups ice**

Freshly grated nutmeg and 6 cinnamon sticks, for garnish

In a blender, combine all of the ingredients except the garnishes and blend until smooth. Pour into chilled mugs and garnish each drink with a pinch of grated nutmeg and a cinnamon stick.

California Caipirinha, p. 102

"Tessa" pitcher and tumbler by Juliska.

PITCHER DRINKS

recipes by duggan mcdonnell

MEET THE MIXOLOGIST

duggan mcdonnell

"My interest in large-format cocktails began when I hosted parties in college," says Duggan McDonnell. "I just wanted to be a good host and create original, fun drinks for my guests." These days he continues to serve exemplary pitcher drinks (made in extra-large shakers), as well as terrific margaritas and caipirinhas, at his Latin-themed San Francisco bar, Cantina. One of the best sellers: the Five-Spice Margarita (p. 97).

santa maria

Wanting to create a cocktail that melds flavors from the Old and New Worlds, McDonnell pulled ingredients from Portugal (port), Mexico (tequila) and the Caribbean (the clove-spiced liqueur Velvet Falernum).

MAKES 8 DRINKS

- 12 ounces blanco tequila
- 6 ounces white port
- 2 ounces Velvet Falernum
- 8 ounces fresh lemon juice
- 2 ounces agave nectar mixed with 2 ounces water
- Ice
- 6 ounces chilled ginger beer
- 8 orange wheels, for garnish

In a large resealable container, combine the first five ingredients; refrigerate until chilled, at least 1 hour. Cover tightly and shake, then pour into an ice-filled pitcher. Strain into ice-filled white wine glasses, top with the ginger beer and garnish.

five-spice margarita

MAKES 8 DRINKS

12 ounces blanco tequila
6 ounces Five-Spice Agave Nectar (below)
4 ounces Cointreau or other triple sec
8 ounces fresh orange juice
5 ounces fresh lime juice
Ice

In a large resealable container, combine all of the ingredients except ice and refrigerate until chilled, at least 1 hour. Cover tightly and shake, then pour into an ice-filled pitcher. Strain into chilled martini glasses.

five-spice agave nectar

In a medium saucepan, bring 16 ounces water to a boil. Add 1 large cinnamon stick, 2 tablespoons black peppercorns, 1 tablespoon white peppercorns, 2 star anise pods, 1 teaspoon whole cloves and a ½-inch piece of fresh ginger, diced. Bring back to a boil and stir in 1 teaspoon sea salt. Add 16 ounces agave nectar and bring to a simmer, stirring frequently. Remove from the heat and let cool. Cover and refrigerate overnight. Strain the syrup into a large jar, cover and refrigerate for up to 3 weeks. Makes about 32 ounces.

Cameron's Cooler

"Free Spirit" juice jug by Rosenthal.

cameron's cooler

Scotch-lover Father Cameron Ayers (a close friend of McDonnell's) challenged the mixologist to come up with a Scotch-based cocktail that was bold and refreshing but stayed true to the whisky's roots.

MAKES 8 DRINKS

- 12 ounces blended Scotch
- 4 ounces dry white wine, such as Sauvignon Blanc
- 4 ounces fresh lemon juice
- 4 ounces Simple Syrup (p. 20)
- Ice
- 8 ounces chilled ginger beer or ginger ale
- Angostura bitters, for garnish

In a large resealable container, combine the first four ingredients; refrigerate for at least 1 hour. Cover and shake, then pour into an ice-filled pitcher. Strain into ice-filled collins glasses, stir in the ginger beer and garnish with dashes of bitters.

pisco punch

In his version of a signature San Francisco drink, Pisco Punch, McDonnell adds limoncello for a bit of citrusy sweetness and ginger beer for spice and effervescence.

MAKES 8 DRINKS

- 8 pineapple chunks (½-inch)
- 12 dashes of Angostura bitters
- 12 ounces pisco, preferably acholado
- 4 ounces limoncello
- 8 ounces fresh orange juice
- 4 ounces Simple Syrup (p. 20)
- 3 ounces fresh lime juice
- Ice
- 8 ounces chilled ginger beer

In a large resealable container, muddle the pineapple and bitters. Add the next five ingredients; refrigerate for at least 1 hour. Cover and shake, then pour into an ice-filled pitcher. Strain into ice-filled rocks glasses; stir in the ginger beer.

Tangerine Collins

"O" pitcher by Riedel; tumblers by Ted Muehling for Lobmeyr.

tangerine collins

Using tangerine juice in place of lemon juice turns the Tom Collins into a great seasonal cocktail. If tangerines aren't available, you can substitute tangelos or clementines.

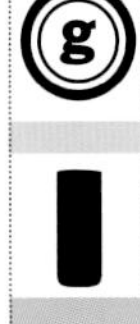

MAKES 8 DRINKS

16 ounces gin
8 ounces tangerine juice
4 ounces Simple Syrup (p. 20)
Ice
8 ounces chilled club soda

In a large resealable container, combine the gin, tangerine juice and Simple Syrup. Refrigerate until chilled, at least 1 hour. Cover tightly and shake, then pour into an ice-filled pitcher. Strain into ice-filled collins or rocks glasses; stir in the club soda.

london dry sangria

With this white sangria, McDonnell makes the Spanish classic global. Grüner Veltliner is a spicy, refreshing Austrian white wine, and London dry gin originated in England.

MAKES 8 DRINKS

12 ounces crisp white wine, such as Grüner Veltliner
6 ounces gin, preferably London dry
8 ounces fresh lemon juice
6 ounces Simple Syrup (p. 20)
10 dashes of orange bitters
Ice
8 ounces chilled ginger beer

In a pitcher, combine all of the ingredients except ice and the ginger beer and stir well. Add ice and stir again. Strain into ice-filled rocks glasses and stir in the ginger beer.

beatnik

This variation on the Manhattan is a nod to the city of San Francisco and its beatnik culture. Averna (a bitter Italian liqueur) is popular in North Beach, the Italian neighborhood where writer Jack Kerouac was known to enjoy a drink.

MAKES 8 DRINKS

24 ounces bourbon
12 ounces tawny port
8 ounces Averna amaro
32 dashes of Peychaud's bitters
Ice
8 orange twists

In a pitcher, combine all of the ingredients except ice and the orange twists and stir well. Add ice and stir again, then strain into chilled martini glasses. Pinch an orange twist over each glass, rub around the rim and add to the drink.

california caipirinha

McDonnell riffs on the caipirinha by embellishing the classic combination of cachaça, sugar and lime with Essensia Orange Muscat from Quady Winery in Madera, California.

MAKES 8 DRINKS

6 limes, cut into eighths
2 tablespoons turbinado sugar
16 ounces cachaça
4 ounces Orange Muscat
4 ounces Simple Syrup (p. 20)
Ice

In a pitcher, muddle the lime wedges with the sugar. Add the cachaça, Orange Muscat and Simple Syrup and stir well. Add ice, stir again and strain the caipirinha into ice-filled rocks glasses.

masala daiquiri

The mix of spices that infuses the rum in this drink is McDonnell's take on masala, a traditional Indian spice blend. Every Christmas he makes a batch of the rum, pours it into mini bottles and gives them as gifts.

MAKES 8 DRINKS

- **16 ounces Masala-Spiced Rum (below)**
- **8 ounces fresh lime juice**
- **6 ounces Simple Syrup (p. 20)**
- **12 dashes of grapefruit bitters, or 8 grapefruit twists for garnish**
- **Ice**
- **8 star anise pods, for garnish (optional)**

In a large resealable container, combine the Masala-Spiced Rum, lime juice, Simple Syrup and bitters, if using. Refrigerate until chilled, at least 1 hour. Cover tightly and shake, then pour into an ice-filled pitcher. Strain into chilled coupes and garnish with the star anise and, if omitting the grapefruit bitters, the grapefruit twists.

masala-spiced rum

Pour one 750-ml bottle white rum into a large jar. Add ¼ cup diced fresh ginger, 2 tablespoons allspice berries, 1 tablespoon each of black peppercorns and lightly crushed cardamom pods, ½ teaspoon whole cloves, 3 medium cinnamon sticks, 3 halved and scraped vanilla beans and their seeds and 1 long strip of orange zest. Stir, cover and refrigerate for 7 to 10 days. Strain the spiced rum into a large glass measuring cup, then pour back into the jar, cover and refrigerate for up to 1 month. Makes about 25 ounces.

Cajun Lemonade

"Barset-Marseille" pitcher and glass by Theresienthal.

cajun lemonade

A salute to the flavors of New Orleans, this cocktail spices up Napoleon House's Pimm's Cup (Pimm's No. 1, lemonade and 7-Up) with a splash of Tabasco and a generous dose of rum or vodka.

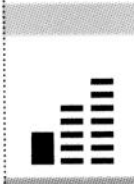

MAKES 8 DRINKS

- 12 ounces white rum or vodka
- 4 ounces Pimm's No. 1
- 8 ounces fresh lemon juice
- 4 ounces Simple Syrup (p. 20)
- ½ tablespoon Tabasco
- Ice
- 8 ounces chilled 7-Up
- Thin lemon wheels, for garnish (optional)

In a large resealable container, combine all of the ingredients except ice, the 7-Up and the lemon wheels. Refrigerate until chilled, at least 1 hour. Cover tightly and shake, then pour into an ice-filled pitcher. Strain into ice-filled rocks glasses, stir in the 7-Up and garnish with lemon wheels.

thieves' punch

While playing with a deck of historical cocktail cards, McDonnell was struck by a card labeled "Thieves' Punch" and decided to create a drink worthy of the name by combining rum and port.

MAKES 8 DRINKS

- 16 ounces white rum
- 5 ounces tawny port
- 10 ounces fresh lime juice
- 5 ounces Simple Syrup (p. 20)
- 20 dashes of Angostura bitters
- Ice

In a pitcher, combine all of the ingredients except ice and stir well. Add ice, stir again and strain into coupes or teacups.

Wager, p. 113

Double old-fashioned glasses by Sagaform.

AFTER-DINNER DRINKS

recipes by jeff grdinich

MEET THE MIXOLOGIST

jeff grdinich

Jeff Grdinich would be a star bartender no matter where he was. To find him mixing drinks in tiny Glen, New Hampshire, at the renovated farmhouse restaurant and bar White Mountain Cider Co., is miraculous. Grdinich launched his career after taking classes with legendary spirits expert Gary Regan. Now he's a pro after-dinner-drink maker (thanks in good part to the mountain town's cold winter nights).

reganomics

The name of this drink refers to famed author and cocktail perfectionist Gary Regan. Grdinich says that deciding on the recipe's proportions was "difficult in a lovable way, much like Gary."

- ¼ ounce green Chartreuse
- Ice
- 1½ ounces dark rum
- 1½ ounces Lustau East India sherry
- 1½ ounces butterscotch schnapps
- 1 ounce apple cider
- 1 orange twist, for garnish

Rinse a chilled snifter with the Chartreuse and pour it out. Fill a cocktail shaker with ice. Add all of the remaining ingredients except the twist and shake well. Strain the drink into the snifter and garnish with the orange twist.

heat of the night

This drink was inspired by the Avenue cocktail in the 1937 Café Royal Cocktail Book, *which combined passion fruit juice and grenadine with Calvados and bourbon.*

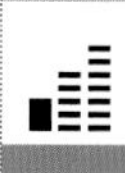

Ice cubes, plus crushed ice
1½ ounces dark rum
1½ ounces St-Germain elderflower liqueur
¾ ounce passion fruit nectar or juice
¼ ounce grenadine, preferably homemade (p. 20)

Fill a cocktail shaker with ice cubes. Add all of the remaining ingredients except crushed ice and shake well. Strain into a crushed ice–filled snifter.

meader made

Grdinich is a big fan of Maine-produced mead (honey wine). He especially likes two dry versions: Fiddler's Reach from Bath and Maine Mead Works's HoneyMaker from Portland.

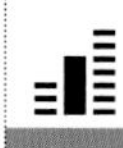

Ice
1½ ounces mead
1 ounce applejack
1 ounce Drambuie (honeyed Scotch-based liqueur)
½ ounce Honey Syrup (p. 54)
½ ounce fresh lemon juice
Dash of Angostura bitters

Fill a cocktail shaker with ice. Add all of the remaining ingredients and shake well. Strain the drink into a chilled white wine glass.

Black & Brown

"Kikatsu" glass from Eastern Accent; lacquer tray by Pacific Connections.

carra-ryed away

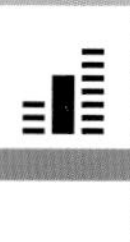

Ice
1½ ounces rye whiskey
1 ounce aquavit
½ ounce Grand Marnier
1 teaspoon amaretto

Fill a pint glass with ice. Add the rye whiskey, aquavit, Grand Marnier and amaretto and stir well. Strain the drink into a chilled coupe.

black & brown

For this drink, Grdinich uses blackberries from his own garden, behind his house.

1 lime wedge and sugar
7 to 10 blackberries
Ice
2 ounces bourbon
1 ounce Navan (vanilla-flavored Cognac-based liqueur)
1 ounce fresh lime juice
Dash of Peychaud's bitters

Moisten the outer rim of a coupe with the lime wedge and coat lightly with sugar. In a cocktail shaker, muddle the blackberries. Add ice and all of the remaining ingredients and shake well. Double strain (p. 17) into the coupe.

north end

The name of this drink, and the Italian limoncello, Fernet-Branca and Prosecco in it, are references to Boston's historically Italian North End neighborhood.

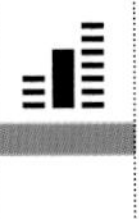

¼ ounce Fernet-Branca (bitter Italian digestif)
Ice
1½ ounces limoncello
½ ounce fresh lemon juice
3 ounces chilled Prosecco

Rinse a chilled flute with the Fernet-Branca and pour it out. Fill a cocktail shaker with ice. Add the limoncello and lemon juice and shake well. Strain into the flute and top with the Prosecco.

60/40

Grdinich created the 60/40 at the New Orleans Tales of the Cocktail festival with the last two ingredients available after everything else had run out: St-Germain elderflower liqueur and Averna amaro.

MAKES 8 DRINKS

12 ounces Averna amaro (bittersweet Italian liqueur)
8 ounces St-Germain elderflower liqueur
Ice

In a jar, combine the amaro and elderflower liqueur and stir well. Cover and refrigerate for at least 1 hour and up to 1 month. Pour into ice-filled rocks glasses.

wager

After winning a bet with a guest about whether bourbon has to be made in Bourbon County, Kentucky (it doesn't), Grdinich designed this cocktail with Bulleit Bourbon from Anderson County.

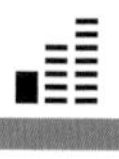

8 to 10 mint leaves, plus 1 large mint sprig for garnish
1 tablespoon turbinado sugar
¼ ounce chilled club soda
Ice
2½ ounces bourbon
2 teaspoons Frangelico
1½ ounces pineapple juice
2 teaspoons pure maple syrup

In a cocktail shaker, muddle the mint leaves and turbinado sugar with the club soda. Add ice and the bourbon, Frangelico, pineapple juice and pure maple syrup and shake well. Double strain (p. 17) into an ice-filled rocks glass and garnish with the mint sprig.

Hat Trick

"Ginevra" Champagne flutes by Alessi.

hat trick

Joe Fee, of Fee Brothers syrup and bitters company, gave Grdinich a bottle of his new rhubarb bitters in 2008. Grdinich concocted this drink with it. The name is a tribute to Mr. Fee, who is known for tipping his ever-present fedora in greeting.

Ice
1½ ounces amontillado sherry
1 ounce Aperol (bitter orange Italian aperitif)
2 dashes of Fee Brothers rhubarb bitters or orange bitters, plus 1 dash for garnish
1½ ounces chilled Prosecco
1 lemon twist wrapped around a pick, for garnish (optional)

Fill a cocktail shaker with ice. Add the sherry, Aperol and 2 dashes of bitters and shake well. Strain into a chilled flute. Top with the Prosecco and garnish with a dash of bitters and the lemon twist.

sloe food

A proud member of the "eco-gastronomic" Slow Food organization, Grdinich designed this cocktail for after-dinner lingering. The Punt e Mes and Frangelico salute Italy, Slow Food's home base.

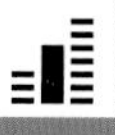

Ice
¾ ounce sloe gin
¾ ounce Punt e Mes (spicy sweet vermouth)
½ ounce Frangelico
½ ounce fresh lemon juice
Dash of Fee Brothers whiskey barrel–aged bitters or Angostura bitters
1 orange twist, for garnish

Fill a cocktail shaker with ice. Add all of the remaining ingredients except the twist and shake well. Strain the drink into a chilled coupe and garnish with the orange twist.

2 if by sweet

Bittermens mole bitters and Cynar, a bitter artichoke liqueur, enhance this drink's chocolaty undertones. Artichoke contains cynarin, a phytochemical that evokes the perception of sweetness in most people.

Ice
1½ ounces reposado tequila
1 ounce white crème de cacao
¾ ounce Cynar
2 dashes of Bittermens Xocolatl Mole Bitters or Angostura bitters

Fill a pint glass with ice. Add all of the remaining ingredients and stir well. Strain the drink into a chilled coupe.

curbside cider

This cocktail features the bitter Italian liqueur Fernet-Branca, made with around 40 different barks, roots, herbs and spices. Fernet-Branca's recipe has been a secret since the first batch was produced in 1845.

1½ ounces rye whiskey
¾ ounce St-Germain elderflower liqueur
¼ ounce Fernet-Branca
4 ounces hot apple cider

In a heatproof mug, mix the rye with the elderflower liqueur and Fernet-Branca. Stir in the cider.

hannah's herb

This hot drink is a nod to Grdinich's bartender friend Chris Hannah of Arnaud's French 75 Bar in New Orleans. The Herbsaint in the recipe is produced by the legendary New Orleans–based Sazerac Company.

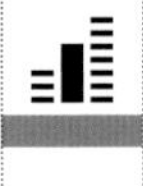

2 ounces Navan (vanilla-flavored Cognac-based liqueur)
½ ounce Herbsaint (anise-flavored liqueur)
4 ounces hot coffee
Dollop of lightly sweetened whipped cream, for garnish

In a heatproof mug, combine the Navan and Herbsaint, then stir in the coffee. Garnish with the whipped cream.

dram delish

For this spiked hot drink, Grdinich favors superindulgent hot cocoa made with cream rather than milk or water.

1½ ounces aged rhum agricole
¾ ounce maraschino liqueur
½ ounce St. Elizabeth Allspice Dram (allspice liqueur)
4 ounces hot chocolate
Dollop of lightly sweetened whipped cream, for garnish
1 star anise pod, for garnish (optional)

In a heatproof mug, mix the rhum agricole with both liqueurs, then stir in the hot chocolate. Garnish with the whipped cream and star anise.

Martinez (left), p. 121

"Newport" martini glass by Theresienthal.

Martini, p. 120

"Sommeliers" martini glass by Riedel.

CLASSICS

compiled by jim meehan

MEET THE MIXOLOGIST

jim meehan

Deputy editor of *FOOD & WINE Cocktails* since 2007, Jim Meehan was a protégé of the pioneering mixologist Audrey Saunders at New York's vaunted Pegu Club. She encouraged him to experiment with spirits and to look to classic cocktail books for inspiration. Meehan, a self-proclaimed lover of cocktail lore, has since taken his talents to PDT, the speakeasy hidden inside the hot dog joint Crif Dogs in New York's East Village.

martini

The original martini, allegedly invented in the U.S. in the 1860s, was made with sweet vermouth. One of the first recipes for a dry martini, made with dry vermouth, appeared in Frank P. Newman's 1904 American Bar.

Ice
3 ounces gin
1 ounce dry vermouth
1 lemon twist, for garnish

Fill a pint glass with ice. Add the gin and vermouth and stir well. Strain into a chilled martini glass or coupe and garnish with the lemon twist.

martinez

The instructions for making the Martinez in O. H. Byron's 1884 Modern Bartenders' Guide *are brief: "Same as Manhattan, only you substitute gin for whisky."*

Ice
1½ ounces Old Tom gin (lightly sweet gin)
1½ ounces Carpano Antica Formula or other sweet vermouth
¼ ounce maraschino liqueur
2 dashes of Angostura bitters
1 orange twist, for garnish

Fill a pint glass with ice. Add all of the remaining ingredients except the twist and stir well. Strain into a chilled martini glass or coupe and garnish with the orange twist.

the crisp

Cocktail historians believe that this drink first appeared in the 1899 edition of Applegreen's Bar Book *as the Crisp Cocktail.*

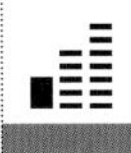

Ice
1¾ ounces gin, preferably Plymouth
1¾ ounces dry vermouth
2 dashes of orange bitters
1 lemon twist, for garnish

Fill a pint glass with ice. Add the gin, vermouth and bitters and stir well. Strain the drink into a chilled coupe and garnish with the lemon twist.

Negroni

"Liquids" martini glass by Gaia & Gino.

negroni

The Negroni is commonly credited to Count Camillo Negroni. He was a Florentine aristocrat who, in the early 1900s, asked for gin in his Americano in addition to the usual sweet vermouth and Campari.

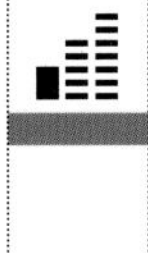

Ice
- **1 ounce gin, preferably London dry**
- **1 ounce Campari**
- **1 ounce sweet vermouth**
- **1 orange twist, for garnish**

Fill a pint glass with ice. Add the gin, Campari and vermouth and stir well. Strain into a chilled martini glass or coupe and garnish with the orange twist.

last word

Bartenders at Seattle's Zig Zag Café purportedly unearthed this Prohibition-era drink from Ted Saucier's 1951 book Bottoms Up.

Ice
- **¾ ounce gin, preferably Tanqueray**
- **¾ ounce green Chartreuse**
- **¾ ounce maraschino liqueur**
- **¾ ounce fresh lime juice**

Fill a cocktail shaker with ice. Add all of the remaining ingredients and shake well. Strain the drink into a chilled coupe.

Mojito (left)

"BAR" glass by LSA from Lekker.

Hemingway Daiquiri

"Mitos" glass by Arik Levy for Květná.

mojito

The oldest-known recipe for the mojito appeared as the Mojo de Ron in a 1929 Cuban guide called Libro de Cocktail (The Cocktail Book).

8 mint leaves, plus 1 mint sprig for garnish
Ice
2 ounces white rum
¾ ounce fresh lime juice
1 ounce Simple Syrup (p. 20)
½ ounce chilled club soda

In a cocktail shaker, muddle the mint leaves. Add ice and the rum, lime juice and Simple Syrup and shake well. Strain into an ice-filled collins glass, stir in the club soda and garnish with the mint sprig.

hemingway daiquiri

In his 2001 book Straight Up or On the Rocks, *William Grimes claims that Ernest Hemingway "often worked his way through about a dozen of these lime slurpees, sometimes ordering doubles, which became known as Papa Dobles."*

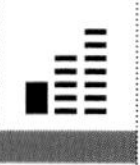

Ice
2 ounces white rum
¾ ounce fresh lime juice
½ ounce fresh grapefruit juice
½ ounce maraschino liqueur
1 lime wheel, for garnish (optional)

Fill a cocktail shaker with ice. Add all of the remaining ingredients except the lime wheel and shake well. Strain into a chilled coupe and garnish with the lime wheel.

margarita

The Picador, a forerunner of the margarita, appeared in England's Café Royal Cocktail Book *in 1937. The margarita allegedly made its print debut in America in December 1953, when* Esquire *named it the "drink of the month."*

1 lime wedge and kosher salt
Ice
2 ounces blanco tequila
¾ ounce Cointreau or other triple sec
¾ ounce fresh lime juice
¼ ounce Simple Syrup (p. 20)

Moisten half of the outer rim of a rocks glass with the lime wedge and coat lightly with salt. Fill a cocktail shaker with ice. Add all of the remaining ingredients and shake well. Fill the rocks glass with ice and strain the drink into the glass.

sidecar

According to Robert Vermeire's 1922 Cocktails: How to Mix Them, *the sidecar was invented by the celebrated bartender MacGarry of London's Buck's Club.*

1 lemon wedge and sugar
Ice
2 ounces Cognac
¾ ounce Cointreau or other triple sec
¾ ounce fresh lemon juice
¼ ounce Simple Syrup (p. 20), optional

Moisten half of the outer rim of a chilled coupe with the lemon wedge and coat lightly with sugar. Fill a cocktail shaker with ice. Add all of the remaining ingredients and shake well. Strain into the coupe.

vieux carré

Stanley Clisby Arthur's 1937 Famous New Orleans Drinks and How to Mix 'Em *attributes this drink to Walter Bergeron, head bartender at the Hotel Monteleone.*

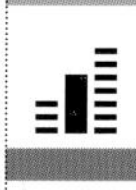

Ice
- 1 ounce Cognac
- 1 ounce rye whiskey
- 1 ounce Carpano Antica Formula or other sweet vermouth
- ¼ ounce Bénédictine (brandy-based herbal liqueur)

Dash of Peychaud's bitters
Dash of Angostura bitters
- 1 lemon twist, for garnish

Fill a pint glass with ice. Add all of the remaining ingredients except the twist and stir well. Strain into a chilled coupe and garnish with the lemon twist.

jack rose

Cocktail book publisher Greg Boehm dates the Jack Rose to the 1910 Jack's Manual.

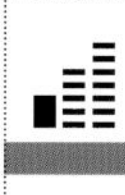

Ice
- 2 ounces bonded apple brandy
- ¾ ounce fresh lemon juice
- ¾ ounce grenadine, preferably homemade (p. 20)

Fill a cocktail shaker with ice. Add the brandy, lemon juice and grenadine and shake well. Strain into a chilled coupe.

Manhattan (left)
and Bronx

Stemware by Peter Behrens from Ameico.

manhattan

The earliest known printed recipe for the Manhattan was published in O. H. Byron's 1884 Modern Bartenders' Guide, *which cites two versions: one made with French vermouth, the other with Italian.*

Ice
- **2 ounces rye whiskey**
- **1 ounce Carpano Antica Formula or other sweet vermouth**
- **2 dashes of Angostura bitters**
- **1 maraschino cherry, for garnish**

Fill a pint glass with ice. Add the rye, vermouth and bitters and stir well. Strain into a chilled coupe and garnish with the cherry.

bronx

In his 1934 book What Shall We Drink?, *Magnus Bredenbek credits this drink to a Bronx restaurateur named Joseph Sormani.*

Ice
- **2 ounces gin**
- **½ ounce sweet vermouth**
- **½ ounce dry vermouth**
- **½ ounce fresh orange juice**

Fill a cocktail shaker with ice. Add all of the remaining ingredients and shake well. Strain into a chilled coupe.

Mint Julep

mint julep

When New Orleans bartender Chris McMillian mixes mint juleps at Bar UnCommon, he recites an ode, written in the 1890s by a Kentucky newspaperman, that calls the cocktail "the zenith of man's pleasure...the very dream of drinks."

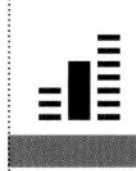

8 mint leaves, plus mint sprigs for garnish
½ ounce Simple Syrup (p. 20)
2 ounces bourbon, preferably overproof
Crushed ice

In a chilled julep cup or fizz glass, muddle the mint leaves and Simple Syrup. Add the bourbon and crushed ice. Set a swizzle stick or bar spoon in the cup and spin between your hands to mix. Top with additional crushed ice and garnish with the mint sprigs.

blood & sand

This drink's name is a tribute to the 1922 silent movie Blood and Sand, *which stars Rudolph Valentino as a poor young Spaniard who eventually becomes a great matador.*

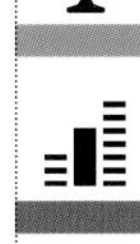

Ice
1½ ounces blended Scotch
¾ ounce cherry liqueur, preferably Heering
¾ ounce sweet vermouth
¾ ounce fresh orange juice

Fill a cocktail shaker with ice. Add all of the remaining ingredients and shake well. Strain the drink into a chilled coupe.

Blackberry-Pineapple Sidecar, p. 143

"Ilya" Champagne coupes by LSA from Lekker.

MIXOLOGISTS' DRINKS

compiled by jim meehan

heather in queue

Jackson Cannon • Eastern Standard, Boston

Cannon uses master formulas to create a wide range of drinks. Heather in Queue's formula is six parts base spirit (gin), three parts fortified wine (vermouth), two parts liqueur (Grand Marnier), one part bitter (Fernet-Branca).

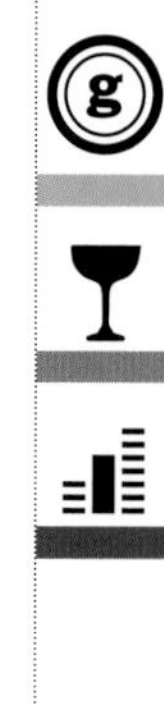

Ice
1½ ounces gin, preferably Plymouth
¾ ounce bianco vermouth (sweet white vermouth)
½ ounce Grand Marnier
¼ ounce Fernet-Branca (bitter Italian digestif)
1 lemon twist, flamed (p. 16), for garnish

Fill a pint glass with ice. Add all of the remaining ingredients except the twist and stir well. Strain the drink into a chilled coupe and garnish with the flamed lemon twist.

dove tail

Toby Maloney • Bradstreet Craftshouse, Minneapolis

"The Dove Tail is nicely balanced with three dashes of orange bitters, but adding a few drops on top of the drink really amplifies its flavor," says Maloney, a cocktail consultant in New York.

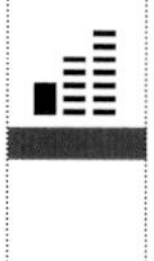

Ice
2 ounces Grand Marnier
1½ ounces fresh grapefruit juice
¾ ounce fresh lemon juice
3 dashes of orange bitters
1 orange twist, for garnish

Fill a cocktail shaker with ice. Add all of the remaining ingredients except the twist and shake well. Strain the drink into a chilled coupe and garnish with the orange twist.

apricino sour

Eric Alperin • The Varnish, Los Angeles

Alperin experimented with grappa as a substitute for South American pisco while creating Italian-inspired drinks at L.A.'s Osteria Mozza.

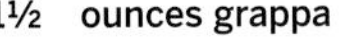

1½ ounces grappa
½ ounce apricot brandy
¾ ounce fresh lemon juice
½ ounce Simple Syrup (p. 20)
1 large egg white
Ice
4 drops of Angostura bitters

In a cocktail shaker, combine the grappa, brandy, lemon juice, Simple Syrup and egg white and shake well. Add ice and shake again. Strain into a chilled coupe, dot with the bitters and draw a straw through the drops.

villa flores

Jonny Raglin • Absinthe Brasserie & Bar, San Francisco

Raglin likes using tequila in cocktails because of the spirit's versatility. In his frothy Villa Flores, muddled jalapeño and ground Sichuan peppercorns magnify the heat of peppery blanco tequila.

1 fresh jalapeño slice, seeded
2 ounces blanco tequila, preferably 7 Leguas
1 large egg white
Ice
1 ounce fresh grapefruit juice
½ teaspoon agave nectar
2 dashes of orange flower water
Pinch of ground Sichuan peppercorns, for garnish

In a cocktail shaker, muddle the jalapeño. Add the tequila and egg white; shake well. Add ice and the juice, agave nectar and flower water; shake again. Strain into a chilled coupe; garnish with the pepper.

Mr. Stair

"Mangold" cocktail glass by Sagaform.

mr. stair

Vincenzo Marianella • Copa d'Oro, Los Angeles

This savory pear sour honors an English schoolmaster who reputedly discovered the Williams pear (a.k.a. the Bartlett pear) around 1765.

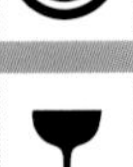

Ice
- 2 ounces pear eau-de-vie
- ¾ ounce St-Germain elderflower liqueur
- ½ ounce fresh lemon juice
- ½ ounce fresh cucumber juice, made from strained pureed cucumber
- ¼ ounce Simple Syrup (p. 20)

Dash of orange bitters
- 1 long, thin cucumber slice threaded onto a skewer, for garnish (optional)

Fill a cocktail shaker with ice. Add all of the remaining ingredients except the cucumber slice and shake well. Strain into a chilled coupe and garnish with the skewered cucumber slice.

sorriso

Francesco Lafranconi • ART Lounge, Seattle

Las Vegas–based cocktail consultant Lafranconi named the Sorriso ("smile" in Italian) as a playful nudge to bartenders to be a little more personable to customers.

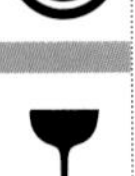

Ice
- 1½ ounces pear vodka
- ¾ ounce gin, preferably Tanqueray No. Ten
- ¾ ounce cream sherry
- ¾ ounce cherry brandy, preferably Luxardo
- 2 dashes of Angostura bitters
- 1 lemon twist, for garnish

Fill a pint glass with ice. Add all of the remaining ingredients except the twist and stir well. Strain into a chilled coupe and garnish with the lemon twist.

céline fizz

Philip Ward • Death & Co., Manhattan

After walking down his tree-lined street in Brooklyn on a spring day last year, Ward came up with this flowery and citrusy cocktail.

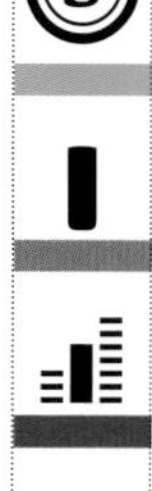

- 2 ounces gin, preferably Plymouth
- ½ ounce St-Germain elderflower liqueur
- ½ ounce fresh grapefruit juice
- ¼ ounce Simple Syrup (p. 20)
- ¼ ounce fresh lemon juice
- Dash of orange bitters
- 1 large egg white
- Ice
- ½ ounce chilled club soda
- 1 grapefruit twist, for garnish

In a cocktail shaker, combine the gin, elderflower liqueur, fresh grapefruit juice, Simple Syrup, fresh lemon juice, orange bitters and egg white and shake well. Add ice to the shaker and shake again. Strain the cocktail into a chilled fizz glass or flute, then top with the club soda. Pinch the grapefruit twist over the drink and rub it around the rim of the glass, then discard the twist.

masala mai tai

Eben Freeman • Tailor, Manhattan

Freeman spikes Victor "Trader Vic" Bergeron's most famous tiki drink, the mai tai, with garam masala. This traditional Indian spice blend includes cloves, coriander and cardamom.

Ice cubes, plus crushed ice
1½ ounces Garam Masala Rum (below)
¾ ounce fresh lime juice
½ ounce orange curaçao or ¼ ounce Grand Marnier mixed with ¼ ounce Simple Syrup (p. 20)
½ ounce orgeat (almond-flavored syrup)
1 mint sprig, for garnish

Fill a cocktail shaker with ice cubes. Add all of the remaining ingredients except crushed ice and the mint and shake well. Strain into a crushed ice–filled rocks glass and garnish with the mint sprig.

garam masala rum

In a skillet, combine 1 heaping teaspoon each of smashed cardamom pods, cumin seeds and crumbled mace with 1 teaspoon each of coriander seeds and peppercorns and ½ teaspoon whole cloves. Toast the spices over moderate heat, shaking the skillet constantly, until fragrant, about 1 minute. Carefully add the hot spices to 1 liter aged rum along with 2 or 3 fresh curry leaves (optional). Cover and refrigerate for 36 hours. Strain the spiced rum into the rum bottle or a large jar, cover and refrigerate for up to 1 month. Shake the bottle before using. Makes about 32 ounces.

Bison Beach

"Ivan" glass by Karim Rashid for Gaia & Gino.

bison beach

John Lermayer • The Florida Room, Miami

Lermayer prefers Żubrówka bison grass vodka for this potent cocktail. Bison grass, which is native to Poland and Belarus, has distinctive vanilla and herbal aromas.

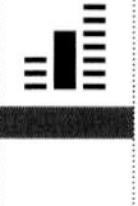

Ice
1½ ounces vodka, preferably bison grass
¾ ounce Aperol (bitter orange Italian aperitif)
2 ounces apple cider
¾ ounce fresh lemon juice
1 orange twist, for garnish

Fill a cocktail shaker with ice. Add the vodka, Aperol, cider and lemon juice and shake well. Strain into a chilled martini glass and garnish with the orange twist.

maximilian affair

Misty Kalkofen • Drink, Boston

As president of the Boston chapter of LUPEC (Ladies United for the Preservation of Endangered Cocktails), Kalkofen combines her interests in vintage drink culture and women's history.

Ice
1 ounce mezcal
1 ounce St-Germain elderflower liqueur
½ ounce Punt e Mes (spicy sweet vermouth)
½ ounce fresh lemon juice

Fill a cocktail shaker with ice. Add all of the remaining ingredients and shake well. Strain into a chilled coupe.

count diablo

Ted Kilgore • Monarch, St. Louis

When asked to create a purple cocktail for a photo shoot at Monarch, Kilgore invented this Negroni-Diablo hybrid.

Ice
1½ ounces blanco tequila
½ ounce crème de cassis
¼ ounce ginger liqueur
¼ ounce Campari
½ ounce fresh lime juice
1 orange twist, flamed (p. 16), for garnish

Fill a cocktail shaker with ice. Add all of the remaining ingredients except the twist and shake well. Strain into a chilled coupe and garnish with the flamed orange twist.

paper plane

Sam Ross • Little Branch, Manhattan

Ross named this drink after singer M.I.A.'s song "Paper Planes," which he listened to while he worked on the recipe.

Ice
¾ ounce bourbon
¾ ounce Nonino Quintessentia amaro (bittersweet Italian liqueur)
¾ ounce Aperol (bitter orange Italian aperitif)
¾ ounce fresh lemon juice

Fill a cocktail shaker with ice. Add all of the remaining ingredients and shake well. Strain into a chilled coupe.

blackberry-pineapple sidecar

Ryan Magarian • The Penthouse, Los Angeles

Magarian, a cocktail consultant based in Portland, Oregon, often focuses on flavor combinations first, then searches for classic cocktail recipes to match. Here he began with the delicious combination of blackberry and pineapple.

7 blackberries
Ice
2 ounces Cognac
½ ounce Cointreau or other triple sec
1½ ounces pineapple juice
½ ounce fresh lemon juice
½ ounce Simple Syrup (p. 20)
1 or 2 pineapple leaves, for garnish (optional)

In a cocktail shaker, muddle the berries. Add ice and all of the remaining ingredients except the garnish; shake well. Strain into a chilled coupe or martini glass and garnish.

oisín's dram

Greg Best • Holeman & Finch Public House, Atlanta

Best named this Irish whiskey-based cocktail after Oisín, a mythological Celtic warrior. Oisín's mother, in some versions of the story, was turned into a deer after he was born.

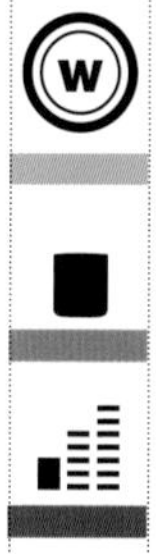

Ice
1½ ounces Irish whiskey, preferably Jameson Gold Reserve
1 ounce tawny port
1 ounce fresh orange juice
4 dashes of Angostura bitters
Pinch of ground cinnamon, for garnish

Fill a cocktail shaker with ice. Add all of the remaining ingredients except the cinnamon and shake well. Strain into an ice-filled rocks glass and garnish with the cinnamon.

Black Friar's Pint

"Maladetta" Champagne flute by Baccarat.

black friar's pint

Jacques Bezuidenhout • Bar Drake, San Francisco

This drink bridges Bezuidenhout's former job pouring pints of Guinness at a pub and his job today mixing martinis and creating cocktails. "When I shake this drink with an egg white, it froths and slowly settles like a mini pint of Guinness," he says.

2 ounces gin
1 ounce Cardamom-Cinnamon Guinness (below)
¾ ounce Lustau East India sherry
Dash of Angostura bitters
1 teaspoon agave nectar
1 large egg white
Ice
Pinch of ground cinnamon, for garnish

In a cocktail shaker, combine all of the ingredients except ice and the cinnamon. Shake well. Add ice and shake again. Strain into a chilled flute and garnish with the cinnamon.

cardamom-cinnamon guinness

In a small saucepan, lightly muddle 2 cardamom pods and 1 medium cinnamon stick. Add 8 ounces Guinness and bring to a boil. Lower the heat and simmer for 1 minute. Let cool, then strain the spiced Guinness into a jar, cover and refrigerate for up to 3 weeks. Makes about 8 ounces.

Hibiscus Swizzle, p. 158

Champagne glasses by Deborah Ehrlich from Takashimaya; cocktail stirrers from Mood Indigo.

MOCKTAILS

recipes by julie reiner

MEET THE MIXOLOGIST

julie reiner

Julie Reiner, who grew up in Hawaii, opened Manhattan's Flatiron Lounge in 2003 with a fresh fruit–forward approach to drinks inspired by the mango trees in her Oahu backyard. Her newest venture is the classically focused Brooklyn cocktail joint Clover Club. Reiner perfected the art of the mocktail mixing alcohol-free drinks for Brooklyn's many hip young mothers-to-be.

faux 75

Reiner created this riff on the classic French 75 on Clover Club's opening night. By removing the gin and replacing the Champagne with a bitter lemon soda, she came up with the ideal drink for her newly pregnant partner, Susan Fedroff.

Ice

1 ounce fresh lemon juice

1 ounce Simple Syrup (p. 20)

3 ounces chilled bitter lemon soda

1 lemon twist, for garnish

Fill a cocktail shaker with ice. Add the lemon juice and Simple Syrup and shake well. Strain into a chilled flute, top with the bitter lemon soda and garnish with the twist.

nola mule

Clover Club's menu is divided into drink categories. The bucks and mules are grouped together because they feature citrus juice and ginger. But, says Reiner, bucks are made with ginger ale, mules with ginger beer.

Ice
1½ ounces pineapple juice
¾ ounce fresh lime juice
1 ounce ginger beer, preferably homemade (below)
¾ ounce Simple Syrup (p. 20)
1 candied ginger slice and 1 lime wheel skewered on a pick, for garnish

Fill a cocktail shaker with ice. Add the pineapple juice, lime juice, ginger beer and Simple Syrup and shake well. Strain into an ice-filled highball glass and garnish with the candied ginger and lime wheel.

ginger beer

In a large saucepan, bring 16 ounces water to a boil. Remove from the heat. In a food processor, puree 4 ounces chopped fresh ginger with 1 tablespoon of the hot water. Add the pureed ginger to the remaining hot water and let stand for 1 hour. Pour through a fine strainer into a glass jar. Add ¾ teapoon fresh lime juice and 1½ teapoons light brown sugar and stir well. Cover and refrigerate for up to 3 weeks. Makes about 16 ounces.

Summer Berry Fizz

"Four Leaf Clover" tumbler from Neue Galerie.

bangkok lemonade

This bubbly lemonade combines two flavors commonly paired in Thai cooking: mint and citrus.

6 to 8 mint leaves, plus 1 mint sprig for garnish
1½ ounces Simple Syrup (p. 20)
Ice
1½ ounces fresh lemon juice
3 ounces bitter lemon soda
1 lemon wheel, for garnish

In a cocktail shaker, muddle the mint leaves with the Simple Syrup. Add ice and the lemon juice and shake well. Double strain (p. 17) into an ice-filled collins glass, stir in the bitter lemon soda and garnish with the mint sprig and lemon wheel.

summer berry fizz

4 raspberries, plus more for garnish
4 blackberries, plus more for garnish
2 strawberries, plus more for garnish
1½ ounces Simple Syrup (p. 20)
Ice
1½ ounces fresh lemon juice
1½ ounces chilled 7-Up

In a cocktail shaker, muddle the 4 raspberries, 4 blackberries and 2 strawberries with the Simple Syrup. Add ice and the lemon juice and shake well. Double strain (p. 17) into an ice-filled highball or collins glass, stir in the 7-Up and garnish with the remaining berries.

sour cherry fizz

Reiner created the original Scotch-based Sour Cherry Fizz at Flatiron Lounge. To bring what she calls "that alcoholic tartness" to the mocktail version, she increased the amount of Sour Cherry Puree and fresh lemon.

1½ ounces Sour Cherry Puree (below)
1½ ounces fresh lemon juice
1 large egg white
Ice
1½ ounces chilled cherry soda
2 maraschino cherries skewered on a pick, for garnish (optional)

In a cocktail shaker, combine the Sour Cherry Puree, lemon juice and egg white and shake well. Add ice and shake again. Strain into an ice-filled highball glass, stir in the cherry soda and garnish with the skewered cherries.

sour cherry puree

In a blender, puree one 13-ounce jar sour cherry preserves with 2 ounces water until smooth. Strain the puree into a jar, cover and refrigerate for up to 3 weeks. Makes about 12 ounces.

juniper & tonic

The spice and orange-peel notes from the Juniper Syrup in this drink evoke the flavors in gin.

Ice

- **1 ounce Juniper Syrup (below)**
- **¾ ounce fresh lime juice**
- **3 ounces chilled tonic water**
- **1 lime wheel, for garnish**

Fill a cocktail shaker with ice. Add the Juniper Syrup and lime juice and shake well. Strain into an ice-filled highball glass, stir in the tonic and garnish with the lime wheel.

MOCKTAILS

juniper syrup

In a small saucepan, muddle one 1.6-ounce jar juniper berries. Add strips of zest from ½ orange, 2 cardamom pods and ½ cup water and bring to a simmer. Stir in ½ cup sugar and simmer for 15 minutes. Let cool, then cover and refrigerate overnight. Strain the syrup into a jar, cover and refrigerate for up to 3 weeks. Makes about 6 ounces.

Lilikoi

"Moya" glass from Lekker.

lilikoi

Smoothies that Reiner made when she lived on Oahu inspired this tangy mocktail, which would be a terrific mimosa stand-in at brunch.

Ice
- **2 ounces Mango-Lilikoi Puree (below)**
- **1 ounce passion fruit nectar or juice**
- **½ ounce Simple Syrup (p. 20)**
- **½ ounce fresh lime juice**
- **½ ounce fresh lemon juice**
- **1 edible orchid, for garnish (optional)**

Fill a cocktail shaker with ice. Add all of the remaining ingredients except the orchid and shake well. Strain into a chilled red wine glass or hurricane glass and garnish with the orchid.

mango-lilikoi puree

Peel and cube 1 mango, then combine in a blender with 3 ounces passion fruit nectar or juice. Blend until smooth. Transfer the puree to a jar, cover and refrigerate for up to 3 days. Makes about 14 ounces.

hibiscus swizzle

Swizzles are drinks that are typically served over crushed ice and churned with a swizzle stick until supercold. Small ice cubes are a fine substitute for crushed ice.

Small ice cubes or crushed ice
3 ounces youngberry juice or 2 ounces mixed-berry juice and 1 ounce pomegranate juice
¾ ounce fresh lemon juice
¾ ounce Hibiscus Syrup (below)
1 ounce chilled club soda

Fill a cocktail shaker with ice. Add the youngberry juice, lemon juice and Hibiscus Syrup and shake well. Strain into an ice-filled highball or collins glass and stir in the club soda.

hibiscus syrup

In a heatproof bowl, combine 8 ounces hot Simple Syrup (p. 20) with 2 hibiscus tea bags and let steep for 5 minutes. Discard the tea bags and let the syrup cool. Transfer the syrup to a jar, cover and refrigerate for up to 2 weeks. Makes about 8 ounces.

lychee fizz

Reiner serves an alcoholic version of this tangy fizz, made with gin, at Flatiron Lounge.

Ice
4 ounces lychee juice or nectar
1 ounce fresh lime juice
3/4 ounce Lemongrass Syrup (p. 37)
1½ ounces chilled club soda
1 lychee (optional) and 1 lime wheel, for garnish

Fill a cocktail shaker with ice. Add the lychee juice, lime juice and Lemongrass Syrup and shake well. Strain into an ice-filled highball glass, stir in the club soda and garnish with the lychee and lime wheel.

cucumber-mint cooler

Four 1-inch cubes of seedless cucumber, plus 1 cucumber spear for garnish
10 mint leaves, plus 1 mint sprig for garnish
2 ounces Simple Syrup (p. 20)
Ice cubes, plus crushed ice
1¼ ounces fresh lime juice

In a cocktail shaker, muddle the cucumber cubes and mint leaves with the Simple Syrup. Add ice cubes and the lime juice and shake well. Double strain (p. 17) into a crushed ice–filled white wine glass and garnish with the cucumber spear and mint sprig.

Lucky Clover

Champagne cup by Lobmeyr from Moss.

lucky clover

As a nonalcoholic option at Clover Club, in the trendy Brooklyn neighborhood of Cobble Hill, Reiner mixes up the bar's signature cocktail, the Clover Club, without the gin and vermouth.

- 2 ounces Raspberry Syrup (below)
- 2 ounces fresh lemon juice
- 2 dashes of orange flower water
- 1 medium egg white
- Ice
- 3 raspberries skewered on a pick, for garnish

In a cocktail shaker, combine all of the ingredients except ice and the skewered raspberries and shake well. Add ice and shake again. Strain into a chilled coupe and garnish with the skewered raspberries.

raspberry syrup

In a saucepan, combine 6 ounces (½ pint) raspberries with ½ cup water and ¾ cup superfine sugar. Cook over low heat for 15 minutes, smashing the raspberries. Remove from the heat and let stand for 30 minutes. Strain the syrup into a jar, cover and refrigerate for up to 4 days. Makes about 8 ounces.

five spice

For Reiner, the holidays aren't complete without a great spiced rum cocktail. The creamy, chai-based Five Spice evokes those flavors.

Ice
- 2 ounces chilled brewed sweetened chai
- 1 ounce milk
- 1 teaspoon pure maple syrup
- ½ teaspoon pure vanilla extract
- 2 dashes of Angostura bitters
- 1 large egg white

Pinch of freshly grated nutmeg, for garnish

Fill a cocktail shaker with ice. Add all of the remaining ingredients except the nutmeg and shake well. Strain into a chilled coupe and garnish with the freshly grated nutmeg.

persephone

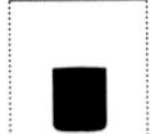

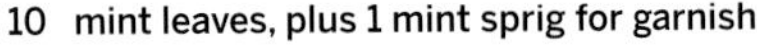

- 10 mint leaves, plus 1 mint sprig for garnish
- 1 ounce Simple Syrup (p. 20)
- 1 teaspoon pomegranate molasses

Ice cubes, plus crushed ice
- 3 ounces pomegranate juice
- ¾ ounce fresh lemon juice
- 4 drops of orange flower water

In a cocktail shaker, muddle the mint leaves with the Simple Syrup and pomegranate molasses. Add ice cubes and all of the remaining ingredients except crushed ice and the mint sprig and shake well. Double strain (p. 17) into a crushed ice–filled rocks glass and garnish with the mint sprig.

sparkling holiday punch

Clover Club serves three different punches, meant for groups of four to six and described like this: "Punch is the granddaddy of all mixed drinks. There are recipes that go as far back as the 1600s."

MAKES 12 TO 14 DRINKS

32 ounces apple cider
¼ cup light brown sugar
15 cloves
10 small cinnamon sticks, plus more for garnish
10 allspice berries
5 cardamom pods
1 whole nutmeg
12 ounces filtered water
1 bottle (750 ml) chilled sparkling pear cider
1 bottle (750 ml) chilled sparkling apple cider
Apple and pear slices and freshly grated nutmeg, for garnish

1. In a large saucepan, combine the apple cider, brown sugar, cloves, 10 cinnamon sticks, allspice, cardamom and nutmeg and bring to a boil. Reduce the heat to low and simmer for 30 minutes. Let cool, then strain the mulled cider into a jar, cover and refrigerate until chilled, or up to 1 week.

2. Pour the filtered water into a wide, shallow plastic container and freeze for at least 6 hours.

3. Pour the mulled cider into a punch bowl and add the ice block. Stir in the sparkling pear and apple ciders, garnish with the apple and pear slices, cinnamon sticks and freshly grated nutmeg and serve in coupes or teacups.

Deviled Eggs with Country Ham, p. 172

"Arcadia" plate by Bodo Sperlein from Clio.

PARTY FOOD

warm marinated olives

Mark Richardson • Seasons Bar & Lounge, San Francisco

The garlicky olives from chef Richardson's bar menu can be ordered alone or as part of "Olives Three Ways." This includes fried blue cheese-stuffed Spanish Queen olives and a kalamata tapenade with sourdough bread crisps.

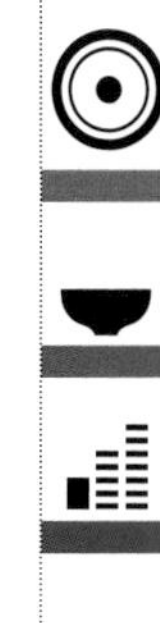

MAKES ABOUT 3½ CUPS

- **1 pound mixed olives, such as kalamata, Picholine and Niçoise**
- **1 cup pearl onions, peeled**
- **1 cup garlic cloves, peeled**
- **8 large thyme sprigs**
- **6 large tarragon sprigs**
- **3 cups extra-virgin olive oil**

In a large saucepan, combine the olives with the pearl onions, garlic, thyme and tarragon. Add the olive oil and bring to a simmer. Cook over moderately low heat until the onions and garlic are tender, about 15 minutes. Discard the herb sprigs. Using a slotted spoon, transfer the olives, onions and garlic to a bowl. Let cool slightly and serve warm.

MAKE AHEAD The olive mixture can be refrigerated for up to 2 weeks. Serve warm or at room temperature.

maple-glazed peanuts & bacon

Meg Grace • The Redhead, Manhattan

"Because everything's better with bacon," reads the menu description for these addictive nuts. The sweet and salty snack has become so popular that the restaurant now sells it online in packs of three 8-ounce mason jars (theredheadnyc.com).

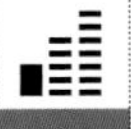

MAKES ABOUT 4 CUPS

- **3 thick slices of bacon (3 ounces)**
- **1 tablespoon thyme leaves, minced**
- **1 tablespoon kosher salt**
- **¾ teaspoon Old Bay Seasoning**
- **½ teaspoon cayenne pepper**
- **½ teaspoon dry mustard**
- **3 cups unsalted roasted peanuts (1 pound)**
- **½ cup pure maple syrup**

1. Preheat the oven to 325°. In a medium skillet, cook the bacon over moderate heat until crisp. Transfer to paper towels to drain, then finely chop.

2. In a medium bowl, mix the thyme, salt, Old Bay, cayenne and dry mustard. Add the peanuts, maple syrup and bacon and toss until the peanuts are evenly coated. Scrape the nuts onto a parchment paper–lined baking sheet and roast for about 30 minutes, stirring once, until the maple syrup has thickened. Let the peanuts cool completely, stirring frequently to break up any large clumps. Transfer the peanuts to glass jars or a large bowl and serve.

MAKE AHEAD The peanuts can be stored in an airtight container for up to 5 days.

fried chickpeas

Seamus Mullen • Boqueria Soho, Manhattan

Mullen learned how to make chickpea fritters at a French-Lebanese restaurant where he worked in college. These smoky, herbed fried chickpeas are a Spanish-inflected spin on that recipe.

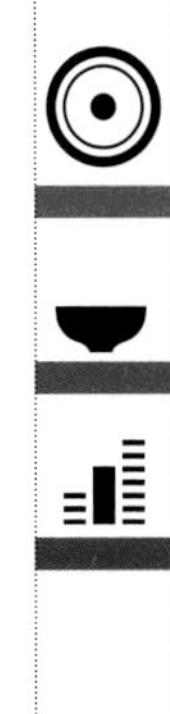

6 SERVINGS

Canola oil, for frying
½ cup chickpea flour or rice flour
1 teaspoon hot pimentón de la Vera (smoked Spanish paprika)
½ teaspoon garlic powder
½ teaspoon onion powder
½ teaspoon ground coriander
Salt
One 15-ounce can chickpeas—drained, rinsed and dried well
1 tablespoon minced flat-leaf parsley
1 tablespoon minced chives
1 tablespoon minced basil
Lemon wedges, for serving

1. In a large saucepan, heat 1 inch of oil to 375°. In a small bowl, mix the chickpea flour with the paprika, garlic powder, onion powder, coriander and ½ teaspoon of salt. Add the chickpeas and toss to coat; shake off any excess flour.

2. Fry the chickpeas, in batches if necessary, until golden and crisp, about 3 minutes. Using a slotted spoon, transfer to paper towels to drain. Season with salt.

3. In a medium bowl, toss the fried chickpeas with the parsley, chives and basil. Serve at once, with lemon wedges.

caramelized onion dip

Michael Schwartz • Michael's Genuine Food & Drink, Miami

Schwartz's ode to Lipton's famous onion soup dip combines caramelized onions, cream cheese, sour cream and mayonnaise.

MAKES ABOUT 4 CUPS

2 tablespoons unsalted butter
2 tablespoons canola oil
5 medium onions, halved and thinly sliced
1 large garlic clove, minced
8 ounces cream cheese, softened
1 cup mayonnaise
1 cup sour cream
Kosher salt and freshly ground pepper
1 teaspoon chopped parsley
Thick-cut potato chips, for serving

1. In a large saucepan, melt the butter in the oil. Add the onions and cook over high heat, stirring frequently, until just softened and beginning to brown, about 10 minutes. Reduce the heat to moderate and cook, stirring frequently, until the onions are golden and softened, about 20 minutes. Add the garlic and cook until fragrant, about 1 minute. Let cool, then coarsely chop the onions.

2. In a standing mixer fitted with the paddle, beat the cream cheese at medium speed until smooth. Beat in the mayonnaise and sour cream. Fold in the onions and season generously with salt and pepper. Scrape into a bowl, cover and refrigerate until chilled. Sprinkle with the parsley and serve with potato chips.

Israeli Hummus with Whole Chickpeas

Napkin by Marimekko.

israeli hummus with whole chickpeas

Michael Solomonov • Zahav, Philadelphia

Before opening Zahav, chef Solomonov took his staff to hummus parlors around Israel in search of the best recipe. The best traditional version, called hummus masabacha, *came from Ali Karavan in Jaffa.*

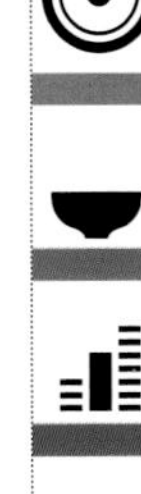

MAKES ABOUT 4 CUPS

- **½ pound dried chickpeas, soaked overnight in water with 1 tablespoon baking soda, then drained and rinsed**
- **7 large garlic cloves, unpeeled**
- **½ cup extra-virgin olive oil**
- **¼ teaspoon ground cumin**
- **½ cup tahini, at room temperature**
- **¼ cup plus 1 tablespoon fresh lemon juice**

Salt

Paprika and chopped parsley, for garnish

Pita bread, for serving

1. In a saucepan, cover the chickpeas and garlic with 2 inches of water; bring to a boil. Simmer over moderately low heat until the chickpeas are tender, about 40 minutes. Drain, reserving ⅔ cup of the cooking water and 2 tablespoons of the chickpeas. Rinse the chickpeas and peel the garlic.

2. In a food processor, puree the chickpeas with ½ cup of the reserved cooking water, ¼ cup of the oil and 6 garlic cloves. Add the cumin and ¼ cup each of the tahini and lemon juice; process until creamy. Season with salt and transfer to a bowl.

3. In the food processor, puree the remaining tahini, oil, lemon juice, reserved cooking water and garlic. Make a well in the hummus and spoon in the tahini. Sprinkle with the reserved chickpeas, paprika and parsley; serve with pita.

deviled eggs with country ham

Ford Fry • JCT. Kitchen & Bar, Atlanta

Chef Fry uses European techniques and flavors at the neighborhood bistro JCT. His deviled eggs get their terrific flavor from goat cheese, Dijon mustard and cornichons, plus a topping of country ham from Benton's in Madisonville, Tennessee.

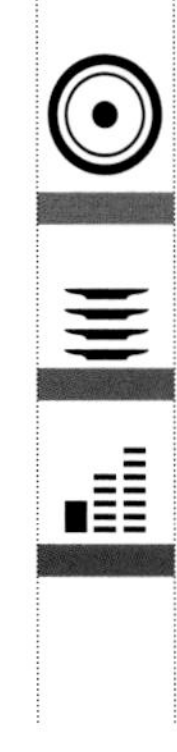

6 TO 8 SERVINGS

- **10 large eggs**
- **¼ cup plus 1 tablespoon mayonnaise**
- **3 cornichons, minced**
- **2 tablespoons goat cheese, at room temperature**
- **2 teaspoons Dijon mustard**
- **1½ teaspoons minced shallot**
- **2 teaspoons snipped chives**
- **Kosher salt and freshly ground pepper**
- **1 ounce thinly sliced country ham or prosciutto, torn into 20 pieces**

1. In a large saucepan, cover the eggs with cold water and bring to a boil over high heat. Remove from the heat and let the eggs stand in the hot water for 10 minutes. Transfer the eggs to an ice water bath until chilled, about 5 minutes.

2. In a medium bowl, mix the mayonnaise, cornichons, goat cheese, mustard, shallot and 1 teaspoon of the chives. Peel the eggs and halve them lengthwise. Add the yolks to the bowl, mix until smooth and season with salt and pepper.

3. Set the egg whites on a serving platter. Scrape the egg yolk mixture into a pastry bag fitted with a large round tip and pipe the filling into the whites; alternatively, spoon in the filling with a teaspoon. Top each egg with a piece of country ham, sprinkle with the remaining 1 teaspoon of chives and serve.

tuna tartare crisps

Lee Hefter • CUT, Las Vegas

For his clever twist on tartare, Hefter tops baguette toasts with sushi-grade tuna, avocado, pickled ginger and a dollop of wasabi mayonnaise.

8 SERVINGS

- 32 thin baguette slices, cut from a medium loaf
- ¼ cup mayonnaise
- 1 teaspoon wasabi paste

Kosher salt and freshly ground pepper

- ½ pound sushi-grade tuna, cut into ¼-inch dice
- 3 tablespoons soy sauce
- 1 Hass avocado, cut into ¼-inch dice
- ⅓ cup finely diced seedless cucumber
- 1 scallion, thinly sliced
- 2 teaspoons chopped pickled ginger

1. Preheat the oven to 350°. Toast the baguette slices on a large baking sheet until light golden and crisp, about 15 minutes. Let cool.

2. In a small bowl, mix the mayonnaise with the wasabi paste and season with salt and pepper.

3. In a medium bowl, gently mix the tuna with the soy sauce, avocado, cucumber, scallion and ginger. Spoon a dollop of the wasabi mayonnaise onto each toast, top with the tuna tartare and serve.

Asparagus Tempura

"Margherita" glass by Richard Ginori for Missoni Home.

asparagus tempura

Michael Schlow • Radius, Boston

This supercrispy tempura from chef Schlow is one of his favorites. "I love anything fried, and it's the perfect cocktail party dish since no knife or fork is necessary," he says. Try serving the tempura with different sauces, like a high-quality soy sauce or curried mayonnaise.

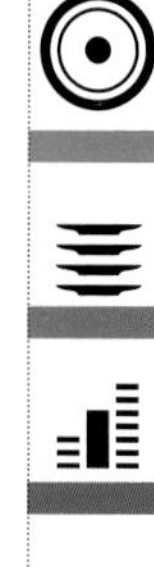

6 SERVINGS

Vegetable oil, for frying
1 cup rice flour
¼ teaspoon baking powder
¼ teaspoon baking soda
1 teaspoon canola oil
1 cup club soda
Salt
24 thin asparagus spears (about 9 ounces), tough bottoms trimmed
Lemon wedges or prepared ponzu sauce, for serving

In a large saucepan, heat 1 inch of vegetable oil to 350°. In a medium bowl, whisk the rice flour with the baking powder, baking soda, canola oil, club soda and 1 teaspoon of salt until smooth. Dip the asparagus in the batter and fry, in batches if necessary, until golden and crisp, about 2 minutes. Drain the asparagus on paper towels and season lightly with salt. Serve at once, with lemon wedges or ponzu sauce.

roast beef & horseradish roll-ups

Chris Pandel • The Bristol, Chicago

Pandel got the idea for this snack from a ham, mustard and pickle roll a friend made for a potluck hosted by Chicago star chef Rick Tramonto. It was the surprise hit of the party.

12 SERVINGS

½ cup *fromage blanc*
1½ tablespoons freshly grated or drained prepared horseradish
1½ teaspoons grainy mustard
1½ teaspoons chopped tarragon
1½ teaspoons snipped chives
Kosher salt and freshly ground pepper
8 thin slices of roast beef (about ½ pound)
1 large dill pickle, quartered

1. In a small bowl, mix the *fromage blanc* with the horseradish, mustard, tarragon and chives; season with salt and pepper.

2. On a work surface, arrange 2 roast beef slices, overlapping the long ends, and spread with one-fourth of the *fromage blanc* mixture. Lay one pickle quarter at a short end and roll the roast beef around the pickle into a tight cylinder. Repeat with the remaining roast beef, *fromage blanc* mixture and pickle quarters. Trim the edges of each roll and slice them 1 inch thick. Arrange on a platter and serve.

queso fundido

Joseph Manzare • Tres Agaves, San Francisco

Chef Manzare and the Tres Agaves staff take regular trips to distilleries in Jalisco, Mexico (tequila capital of the world). They start most of their meals with queso fundido, *Mexico's version of cheese fondue.*

4 SERVINGS

1 fresh chorizo (about 4 ounces)
1 teaspoon canola oil
½ cup fresh or thawed frozen corn kernels
½ medium Anaheim chile or 1 jalapeño, seeded and thinly sliced crosswise
Kosher salt
2 cups shredded Monterey Jack cheese
1 cup shredded sharp cheddar cheese
Tortilla chips or warm corn tortillas, for serving

1. Preheat the oven to 400°. On a rimmed baking sheet, roast the chorizo for about 15 minutes, until browned and cooked through. Let cool, then coarsely chop.

2. In a small skillet, heat the oil. Add the corn and chile and cook over moderately high heat until browned in spots, about 3 minutes. Remove from the heat and stir in the chorizo. Season with salt.

3. Spray a 6-inch cast-iron skillet or small enameled cast-iron casserole with vegetable oil cooking spray. Heat the skillet in the oven for 5 minutes, until hot. Sprinkle half of the Monterey Jack and cheddar in the skillet, top with the chorizo mixture and sprinkle with the remaining cheese. Bake for about 5 minutes, until the cheese is melted and bubbly around the edge. Serve at once, with tortilla chips.

Polpette in Spicy Tomato Sauce

polpette in spicy tomato sauce

Ruggero Gadaldi • Beretta, San Francisco

A die-hard Sopranos *fan, chef Gadaldi says that the TV show inspires many of his hearty Italian dishes, including these* polpette *(meatballs).*

12 SERVINGS

- 1 pound ground veal
- ½ pound sweet Italian sausage, casings removed
- 1 cup dry bread crumbs
- ½ cup whole milk
- 3 garlic cloves, minced
- 2 tablespoons chopped flat-leaf parsley
- 2 large egg whites
- 1 tablespoon tomato paste
- ½ cup freshly grated Pecorino Romano cheese, plus more for sprinkling
- Salt and freshly ground pepper
- 2½ cups prepared tomato sauce
- Large pinch of crushed red pepper

1. Preheat the oven to 350°. In a bowl, mix the veal with the sausage meat, bread crumbs, milk, garlic, chopped parsley, egg whites, tomato paste and ½ cup of pecorino; season with salt and pepper. Roll into 1½-inch meatballs. Bake the meatballs on a lightly oiled baking sheet for about 30 minutes, until browned and cooked through.

2. In a large saucepan, season the tomato sauce with the crushed red pepper. Add the meatballs and simmer until the sauce is slightly thickened, about 8 minutes. Sprinkle with pecorino cheese and serve.

coconut shrimp beignets with pepper jelly dipping sauce

Allison Vines-Rushing & Slade Rushing • MiLa, New Orleans

This bar snack is an ingenious combination of two classic fried foods: crisp coconut shrimp and beignets (fritters). Whisking both beer and egg into the batter makes for a crust that's crunchy on the outside and fluffy on the inside.

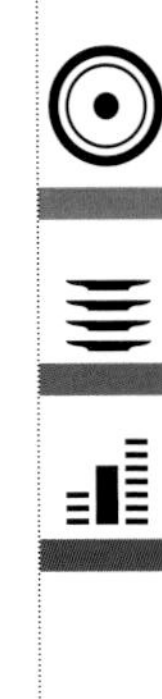

8 SERVINGS

One 10-ounce jar red pepper jelly
- ¼ cup Creole mustard or grainy mustard
- 1 tablespoon Champagne vinegar or white wine vinegar

Vegetable oil, for frying
- 2 cups all-purpose flour
- 3 scallions, thinly sliced
- 1 cup unsweetened shredded coconut
- 1 tablespoon baking powder
- 1 tablespoon sugar
- 2 teaspoons salt
- 1 teaspoon freshly ground pepper

One 12-ounce bottle amber beer
- 1 large egg, lightly beaten
- 1½ pounds large shrimp, shelled and deveined, tails left on

1. In a bowl, whisk the pepper jelly with the mustard and vinegar until smooth.

2. In a large saucepan, heat 1½ inches of vegetable oil to 350°. In a bowl, mix the flour with the scallions, coconut, baking powder, sugar, salt and pepper. Whisk in the beer and egg to form a thick batter.

3. Working in batches, dip the shrimp in the batter (don't shake off the excess) and fry over moderate heat, turning once, until golden and crisp, about 3 minutes. Using a slotted spoon, transfer the shrimp to paper towels to drain. Serve with the pepper jelly sauce.

danger tots

Jane Danger • PDT, Manhattan

These Tots aren't on PDT's menu, but insiders know to ask for them. PDT usually serves the toppings (cheddar cheese, bacon, sour cream, guacamole and more) on hot dogs.

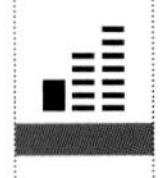

6 SERVINGS

Vegetable oil, for frying
One 32-ounce package frozen Tater Tots
Kosher salt
1½ cups shredded sharp cheddar cheese
½ cup prepared guacamole
¼ cup sour cream
3 slices of bacon, cooked until crisp and crumbled
1 plum tomato—halved, seeded and cut into ¼-inch dice
1 jalapeño, thinly sliced

1. In a large, deep skillet, heat 1 inch of vegetable oil to 400°. Working in batches, fry the Tater Tots, stirring once or twice, until golden and crisp, about 3 minutes. Transfer to paper towels to drain and season with salt.

2. Preheat the broiler. Pile the fried Tater Tots on an ovenproof serving plate and sprinkle with the cheese. Broil 2 inches from the heat for about 1 minute, or until the cheese is melted. Spoon the guacamole and sour cream over the Tater Tots, sprinkle with the bacon, tomato and jalapeño and serve.

Shrimp Salad Slider

Napkin by Iittala.

shrimp salad sliders

Craig Rivard • Clover Club, Brooklyn, New York

The Clover Club menu describes these mini sandwiches as "lobster rolls during a recession." At Clover Club, the sliders come two to an order, and are made with freshly baked, scooped-out Parker House rolls.

10 SERVINGS

1 pound cooked large shrimp, coarsely chopped
1 celery rib, finely chopped
½ cup mayonnaise
2½ tablespoons fresh lemon juice
2 tablespoons snipped chives
1 tablespoon minced flat-leaf parsley
1 tablespoon chopped basil
Kosher salt and freshly ground pepper
Ten 3-inch round white dinner rolls or sourdough rolls
4 tablespoons unsalted butter, softened

1. Preheat the oven to 325°. In a medium bowl, mix the shrimp with the celery, mayonnaise, lemon juice, chives, parsley and basil; season the shrimp salad with salt and pepper.

2. Using a paring knife, cut a 2-inch round from the top of each roll. Discard the filling from the rolls, set the rolls on a baking sheet and warm in the oven, about 5 minutes. Butter the inside of the rolls and fill with the shrimp salad. Top with the lids and serve.

ham & cheese torta with homemade honey mustard

Barbara Lynch • Drink, Boston

At Lynch's new cocktail-focused bar, modernized Prohibition-era drinks are accompanied by bite-size dishes like this buttery-crisp puff pastry torta.

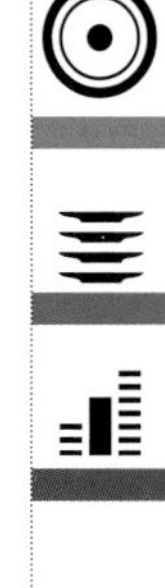

8 TO 10 SERVINGS

- 1 tablespoon extra-virgin olive oil
- 1 small onion, halved and thinly sliced
- ¼ cup plus 2 tablespoons honey
- 2½ tablespoons Dijon mustard
- Two 14-ounce packages frozen all-butter puff pastry, thawed but cold
- 1 pound thinly sliced smoked ham
- 2 cups shredded Gruyère cheese
- 1 large egg, lightly beaten
- ½ teaspoon coarse sea salt

1. Preheat the oven to 375°. In a medium skillet, heat the oil. Add the onion and cook over moderate heat, stirring, until softened, about 6 minutes. Add the honey and mustard and cook, stirring, until thickened and deep amber, about 15 minutes. Puree in a food processor until almost smooth.

2. Lay 1 sheet of the puff pastry on a parchment paper–lined baking sheet. Brush with the honey mustard, leaving a ½-inch border all around. Arrange the ham over the mustard, then the cheese. Top with the remaining pastry sheet. Pinch the edges together to seal and fold over to form a ½-inch-wide border; crimp with a fork. Brush the top with the beaten egg and sprinkle with the salt. Using a fork, poke a few holes in the pastry. Bake for about 1 hour, until golden. Let stand for 30 minutes. Cut into rectangles and serve warm.

butter lettuce "wedge" salad

Michael Corvino • Urban Farmer, Portland, Oregon

Urban Farmer upgrades the classic iceberg wedge salad by adding crispy pork rinds, avocado and hot pickled peppers to the mix, and finishing the dish with a sunny-side up duck egg.

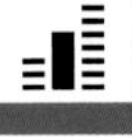

4 SERVINGS

- ¼ cup beef demiglace (available at specialty food stores)
- 1 tablespoon prepared roasted garlic puree
- 1 tablespoon minced hot Italian pickled peppers
- 1 tablespoon extra-virgin olive oil
- 1 tablespoon red wine vinegar
- 3 slices of pumpernickel rye bread, crusts removed, bread cut into ½-inch dice
- One 1-ounce piece of pancetta, cut into ¼-inch dice
- 1 head butter lettuce, quartered
- 4 ounces blue cheese, crumbled (1 cup)
- 1 Hass avocado, cut into ½-inch dice
- 2 tablespoons snipped chives

1. Preheat the oven to 350°. In a small bowl, whisk the demiglace with the garlic puree, hot peppers, olive oil and vinegar.

2. Spread the bread cubes on a baking sheet and toast in the oven for about 15 minutes, tossing once or twice, until crisp. Let cool.

3. In a small skillet, cook the pancetta over moderate heat, stirring, until golden and crisp, about 6 minutes. Transfer to paper towels to drain.

4. In a bowl, toss the lettuce with the garlic dressing, blue cheese, avocado and croutons. Transfer to plates, sprinkle with the pancetta and chives and serve.

twice-baked cheese & scallion potatoes

Donald Link • Cochon, New Orleans

When Link bakes these cheesy, cayenne-spiked potatoes for himself, he increases the amount of butter and salt because, he says, "They're the two most important ingredients for making really good stuffed or mashed potatoes."

8 SERVINGS

4 medium baking potatoes
1½ teaspoons extra-virgin olive oil
Kosher salt and freshly ground black pepper
3 scallions, thinly sliced
4 ounces sharp cheddar cheese, coarsely shredded (1½ cups)
¼ cup sour cream
4 tablespoons unsalted butter, softened
Pinch of cayenne pepper
Pinch of freshly grated nutmeg

1. Preheat the oven to 375°. Rub the potatoes with the olive oil and season with salt and black pepper. Bake directly on the oven rack for about 1 hour, or until tender. Let stand until warm. Leave the oven on.

2. Halve the potatoes lengthwise. Scoop the potato flesh into a bowl, leaving a ¼-inch-thick shell. Add the scallions, cheddar, sour cream, butter, cayenne and nutmeg and mash until smooth; season with salt and black pepper.

3. Scoop the filling into the potato skins and bake for about 25 minutes, until heated through and golden on top. Serve the potatoes hot.

carbonara pizza

Frank Bonanno • Osteria Marco, Denver

Bonanno loves pasta carbonara. He transforms the dish into a pizza by topping a thin-crusted pie with sunny-side up eggs and pancetta.

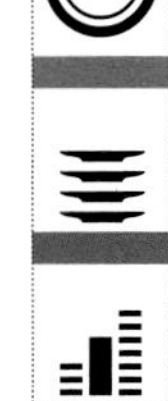

4 SERVINGS

One ½-pound ball of fresh or thawed frozen pizza dough
¼ cup mascarpone cheese
2 tablespoons freshly grated Pecorino Romano cheese
2 thick slices of pancetta, cut into ¼-inch dice
Freshly ground pepper
2 large eggs
Kosher salt
1 tablespoon coarsely chopped flat-leaf parsley

1. Preheat the oven to 450°. Set a pizza stone or inverted baking sheet in the middle of the oven to preheat. On a lightly floured surface, roll out the dough to a 12-inch round and transfer to a lightly floured pizza peel.

2. Spread the mascarpone on the dough, leaving a ½-inch border. Sprinkle with the pecorino and pancetta and season with pepper. Slide the pizza onto the stone and bake for about 6 minutes, until the crust is set and the topping begins to bubble. Crack the eggs over the pizza and bake for about 6 minutes longer, until the crust is golden, the egg whites are set and the yolks are still runny. Season the eggs lightly with salt, sprinkle with the parsley and serve.

Banger & Egg Sandwich

"Pierrot" plate by Richard Ginori for Missoni Home.

banger & egg sandwiches

Christopher Keating • J-Bar, Aspen, Colorado

Members and fans of Aspen's rugby team—fixtures at J-Bar—have a reputation for badgering the chef to put English dishes on the menu. They insisted on bangers (British slang for sausages) and eggs, which Keating serves on toast with sharp cheddar.

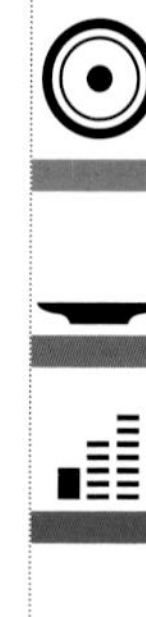

4 SERVINGS

- 1 teaspoon vegetable oil
- 8 country sausages, such as fresh breakfast sausages
- 2 plum tomatoes, halved lengthwise
- Kosher salt and freshly ground pepper
- 2 tablespoons unsalted butter
- 8 large eggs
- 8 slices of potato bread, toasted
- 4 ounces sharp cheddar cheese, thinly sliced
- 1 tablespoon chopped flat-leaf parsley

1. In a large cast-iron skillet, heat the oil. Add the sausages and cook over moderate heat, turning, until browned and cooked through, about 8 minutes. Let cool slightly. Halve the sausages lengthwise and cook cut side down over moderate heat until browned, about 2 minutes. Transfer to a plate.

2. Season the tomatoes with salt and pepper, add them to the skillet cut side down and cook over high heat until browned, about 3 minutes. Transfer the tomatoes to a plate.

3. Melt 1 tablespoon of the butter in each of 2 skillets. Fry 4 eggs in each skillet over moderate heat until slightly runny in the center, about 4 minutes. Season with salt and pepper. Set 2 eggs on each of 4 toast slices. Top with the cheese and sausages, sprinkle with the parsley and close the sandwiches. Serve with the tomatoes.

oyster pan roast with tarragon toasts

April Bloomfield • The John Dory, Manhattan

At her new seafood-centric restaurant, Bloomfield updates fish house favorites like this pan roast of oysters in a seasoned cream sauce.

4 SERVINGS

- **1 tablespoon extra-virgin olive oil**
- **½ small onion, minced**
- **2 garlic cloves, 1 clove minced**
- **¼ cup dry vermouth**
- **2 dozen oysters, such as Wellfleet, shucked, ¼ cup oyster liquor reserved**
- **¾ cup water**
- **1 cup heavy cream**
- **1½ teaspoons fresh lemon juice**
- **Kosher salt**
- **4 tablespoons unsalted butter, softened**
- **¼ cup tarragon, minced**
- **8 baguette slices, toasted**

1. In a large saucepan, heat the oil. Add the onion and minced garlic; cook over moderate heat until softened, 5 minutes. Add the vermouth; boil over moderately high heat until reduced by half, about 2 minutes. Add the oyster liquor and water and simmer for 3 minutes. Add the cream and simmer over moderate heat until the sauce coats a spoon, 5 minutes. Remove from the heat. Add 1 teaspoon of the lemon juice; season with salt.

2. In a bowl, mix the butter with the tarragon and the remaining ½ teaspoon of lemon juice; season with salt. Lightly rub the toasts with the garlic clove and spread with the tarragon butter.

3. Add the oysters to the sauce. Cook over moderately low heat until warmed through, 2 minutes. Serve with the toasts.

honey-whiskey chicken wings

Jonathan McDonald • Pub & Kitchen, Philadelphia

McDonald sprinkles chile-spiced sugar on these wings to give them a touch of heat. He recommends serving the wings with a Manhattan or any bourbon cocktail that isn't overly sweet.

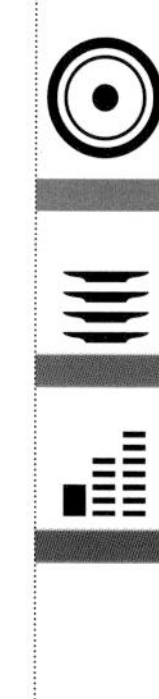

6 SERVINGS

- **2 dozen whole chicken wings, tips left on**
- **Kosher salt and freshly ground pepper**
- **¾ cup honey**
- **¼ cup whiskey**
- **¼ cup plus 2 tablespoons Dijon mustard**
- **2 tablespoons turbinado sugar**
- **2 tablespoons finely grated lime zest (from 2 limes)**
- **1½ tablespoons New Mexico or ancho chile powder**

1. Preheat the oven to 450°. Arrange the wings in a single layer on 2 rimmed baking sheets and season with salt and pepper. Roast for about 40 minutes, until crisp, golden and cooked through.

2. In a small saucepan, whisk the honey with the whiskey and bring to a simmer over moderately high heat. Off the heat, whisk in the mustard.

3. In a bowl, mix the sugar with the zest, chile powder and 1½ teaspoons of salt.

4. Transfer the wings to a large bowl. Pour the sauce on top and toss to coat. Transfer the wings to a platter, sprinkle with some of the spiced sugar and serve. (Use any remaining spiced sugar to season roast chicken or pork.)

Pulled Chicken & Grilled Corn Tacos

Platter by Heath Ceramics; "Mauste" napkin by Marimekko.

pulled chicken & grilled corn tacos

Ryan Pera • Treehouse at the Grove, Houston

The cilantro used in chef Pera's tacos comes from an herb garden next to the open-air, eco-friendly Treehouse bar.

4 SERVINGS

- 2 ears of corn, shucked
- 1 chipotle in adobo, minced to a paste
- 2 tablespoons extra-virgin olive oil
- 2 garlic cloves, minced
- 1 medium shallot, minced
- 1½ cups shredded roast chicken
- 2 tablespoons coarsely chopped cilantro
- Kosher salt and freshly ground pepper
- Eight 6-inch corn tortillas, warmed
- 3 tablespoons crumbled queso fresco or feta cheese
- Prepared tomatillo salsa, for serving

1. Light a grill or preheat a grill pan. Rub the corn with the chipotle paste and grill over moderately high heat, turning, until lightly charred all over, about 4 minutes total. Let cool slightly, then cut the kernels off the cob.

2. In a medium skillet, heat the olive oil. Add the garlic and shallot and cook over moderate heat until softened, about 2 minutes. Add the shredded chicken and cook until heated through, about 1 minute. Stir in the corn and cilantro and season with salt and pepper.

3. Fill the tortillas with the chicken and corn. Sprinkle with the queso fresco, drizzle with tomatillo salsa and serve.

BLT Chili

Bowl from ABC Home; spoon from Ochre; "Black Forest" salad plate by Dibbern.

blt chili

Laurent Tourondel • BLT Burger, Las Vegas

Chef Laurent Tourondel uses a cured pork sausage flavored with fennel seed, anise and garlic in this hearty chili.

8 SERVINGS

2 tablespoons vegetable oil
3 pounds pork sausage, casings removed
2 medium onions, cut into ¼-inch dice
1 red bell pepper, cut into ¼-inch dice
6 garlic cloves, minced
2 tablespoons tomato paste
2 tablespoons chili powder
2 tablespoons sweet paprika
1 tablespoon cumin seeds
1 tablespoon dried oregano
Two 28-ounce cans diced tomatoes
Two 16-ounce cans kidney beans, drained
1 cup corn kernels
4 cups water
Kosher salt and freshly ground pepper
Shredded cheddar cheese, sour cream, chopped onion, pickled jalapeños and hot sauce, for serving

In an enameled cast-iron casserole, heat the oil. Add the sausage and cook over high heat, breaking it up, until browned, about 15 minutes. Add the onions, bell pepper and garlic; cook over moderately high heat, stirring, until the onion is translucent, 8 minutes. Add the tomato paste and cook for 3 minutes. Add the chili powder, paprika, cumin and oregano and cook for 1 minute. Add the tomatoes, beans, corn and water and cook over moderately low heat, stirring occasionally, until thickened, about 1 hour. Season with salt and pepper. Serve the chili with cheddar, sour cream, onion, jalapeños and hot sauce.

grilled lamb skewers with cucumber salad

Andy Ricker • Pok Pok, Portland, Oregon

These fiery kebabs were inspired by lamb skewers that Ricker bought from street vendors in China's Yunnan Province. "They were the perfect snack for chilly winter evenings: spicy, hot and eaten right off the stick," says Ricker.

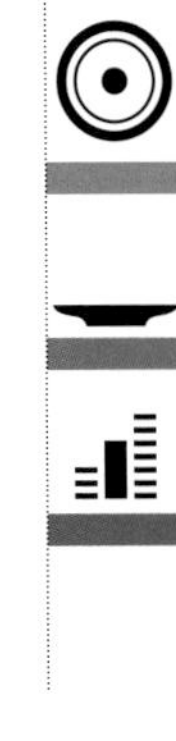

6 SERVINGS

- 2 tablespoons cumin seeds
- 2 tablespoons coriander seeds
- 1½ teaspoons red chile powder
- ¾ teaspoon Sichuan peppercorns
- 1½ teaspoons caraway seeds
- 1 medium seedless cucumber, diced
- 1 pint cherry tomatoes, halved
- 1 small red onion, cut into ½-inch dice
- 4 pickled garlic cloves, thinly sliced, plus 2 tablespoons pickling liquid
- ¼ cup distilled white vinegar
- Kosher salt and freshly ground pepper
- 2 pounds trimmed boneless leg of lamb, cut into 1-inch dice

1. In a skillet, toast the cumin, coriander, chile powder and Sichuan peppercorns over moderate heat, shaking the pan, until fragrant, about 2 minutes. Transfer to a spice grinder and let cool. Finely grind the spices and transfer to a bowl.

2. Toast the caraway in the skillet over moderate heat until fragrant, 2 minutes. Transfer to a bowl; add the cucumber, tomatoes, onion, garlic, pickling liquid and vinegar. Season with salt and pepper.

3. Light a grill. Thread the lamb onto metal skewers. Season with salt and pepper and then the ground spices. Grill over moderately high heat until well browned outside and pink inside, 3 minutes per side. Transfer to a platter and serve with the cucumber salad.

eggplant, cheese & pancetta calzones

Kevin Delk • Mario's Double Daughter's Salotto, Denver

Mario's Double Daughter's is known for pizzas and calzones like this one, which combines tender roasted eggplant, salty pancetta and two types of cheese. One of their less traditional calzones includes roast leg of lamb, feta, mint and golden raisins.

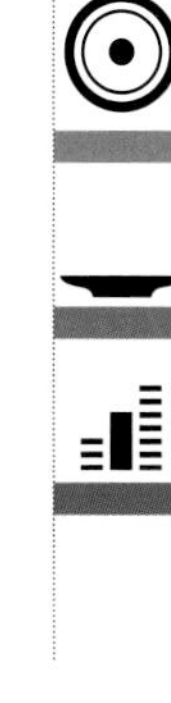

4 SERVINGS

½ medium eggplant (¾ pound)
One 2-ounce piece of pancetta, diced
½ cup finely diced onion
1 small garlic clove, minced
¾ cup canned whole tomatoes, crushed
1 tablespoon minced basil
1 teaspoon minced oregano
Pinch of crushed red pepper
Kosher salt and freshly ground black pepper
Two 10-ounce balls of fresh or thawed frozen pizza dough, halved
¼ cup ricotta cheese
2 ounces fresh mozzarella cheese, diced

1. Preheat the oven to 375°. On a baking sheet, roast the eggplant for about 30 minutes, until tender. Discard the skin; coarsely chop the flesh.

2. In a skillet, cook the pancetta over moderate heat until crisp, 10 minutes. Drain on paper towels. Cook the onion, garlic and eggplant in the skillet over moderate heat until the onion is tender, 5 minutes. Add the tomatoes, herbs and red pepper; cook over moderately high heat until thickened, 6 minutes. Season with salt and pepper; let cool slightly.

3. On a floured surface, roll out the dough halves to 6-inch rounds. Spread the filling over, leaving a ½-inch border. Top with the pancetta, ricotta and mozzarella. Fold the dough over; crimp the edges to seal. Bake on a baking sheet for 25 minutes, until golden. Let cool slightly; serve.

Uncle Louie Burger

PARTY FOOD

uncle louie burgers

Carolynn Spence • Bar Marmont, Los Angeles

Named for a line cook who added bacon, avocado and Russian dressing to the house burger, the Uncle Louie was once available only to staffers. Then a manager ordered a burger "Louie-style" in front of a few of the bar's regulars and word got out. By popular demand, it was added to the menu.

4 SERVINGS

- ¼ cup plus 2 tablespoons ketchup
- ¼ cup mayonnaise
- ¼ cup finely chopped bread-and-butter pickles
- 2 teaspoons distilled white vinegar
- ½ teaspoon dry mustard
- ¼ teaspoon cayenne pepper
- ¼ teaspoon Old Bay Seasoning
- Kosher salt and freshly ground black pepper
- 2 pounds ground chuck
- 4 hamburger buns, preferably brioche, split and toasted
- Butter lettuce, sliced tomato, sliced cheddar cheese, crisp bacon and sliced avocado, for serving

1. In a medium bowl, mix the ketchup with the mayonnaise, pickles, vinegar, dry mustard, cayenne and Old Bay; season with salt and pepper. Refrigerate until ready to serve.

2. Light a grill or preheat a grill pan. In a large bowl, season the chuck with 2 teaspoons of kosher salt and ½ teaspoon of pepper. Gently mix the seasonings into the meat and shape into four ¾-inch-thick patties. Grill the hamburgers over moderately high heat for about 4 minutes per side for medium-rare. Set the burgers on the buns, top with the ketchup sauce, lettuce, tomato, cheese, bacon and avocado and serve.

two-day marinated fried chicken

Art Smith • Art & Soul, Washington, DC

This tender, juicy fried chicken is marinated twice: first in a brine, then in a Tabasco-buttermilk mixture. Smith learned to brine chicken from his good friend Scott Peacock, chef at Watershed in Decatur, Georgia.

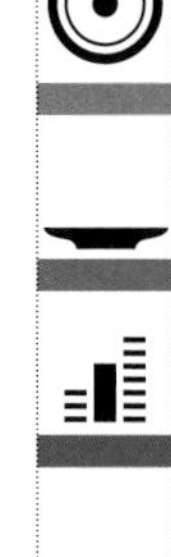

4 SERVINGS

½ cup plus 1 teaspoon kosher salt
4 quarts cold water
One 4-pound chicken, cut into 8 pieces
1 quart buttermilk
2 tablespoons Tabasco
2 cups all-purpose flour
1 tablespoon baking powder
1½ teaspoons garlic powder
1½ teaspoons Old Bay Seasoning
1 teaspoon cayenne pepper
1 teaspoon freshly ground black pepper
Vegetable oil, for frying

1. In a pot, dissolve ½ cup of the salt in the water. Submerge the chicken in the brine; refrigerate overnight.

2. Drain and rinse the chicken. Rinse out the pot. Add the buttermilk and Tabasco, submerge the chicken in the buttermilk and refrigerate for 8 hours or overnight.

3. In a shallow bowl, mix the flour, baking powder, garlic powder, Old Bay, cayenne, black pepper and the remaining 1 teaspoon of salt. Shake the excess marinade off the chicken, then dredge in the flour. Dip the chicken back into the buttermilk and coat again in the flour.

4. Meanwhile, in a large cast-iron skillet, heat 1 inch of vegetable oil to 375°. Fry the chicken in batches until golden and cooked through, about 6 minutes per side. Drain on paper towels and serve.

tagliata of porcini-rubbed rib eye

Matt Molina • Osteria Mozza, Los Angeles

A porcini spice rub from Mario Batali's Babbo Cookbook *forms the sweet, earthy crust on this rib eye. "Tagliata," from the Italian* tagliare, *means "to cut," and refers to the Italian custom of serving steak sliced.*

4 TO 6 SERVINGS

- ¾ ounce dried porcini mushrooms, finely ground in a spice grinder
- 2 tablespoons sugar
- 1 tablespoon kosher salt
- 1 tablespoon freshly ground black pepper
- 1 tablespoon crushed red pepper
- 5 garlic cloves, minced
- ¼ cup extra-virgin olive oil
- One 3½-pound bone-in rib eye steak (3 inches thick)
- Balsamic vinegar, for drizzling

1. In a bowl, mix the porcini powder, sugar, salt, black pepper, red pepper, garlic and olive oil. Rub the paste all over the steak. Cover and refrigerate for 12 hours or overnight. Scrape off the excess paste; let the steak stand at room temperature for 1 hour.

2. Light a grill, or heat a grill pan and preheat the oven to 450°. Grill the steak over medium heat for about 25 minutes per side, until crusty and brown and an instant-read thermometer inserted in the center registers 125° for medium-rare. Alternatively, brown the steak in a grill pan over moderately high heat, about 12 minutes per side, then roast in the oven for about 40 minutes. Let the steak stand for 15 minutes.

3. Slice the meat across the grain, drizzle lightly with balsamic vinegar and serve with an arugula salad.

top 100 bars

A listing of the country's best bars, lounges and restaurants, many of which contributed the incredible cocktails and bar snacks in this book.

ATLANTA

Holeman & Finch Public House
2277 Peachtree Rd.
404-948-1175
From the team behind Restaurant Eugene, this gastropub serves Southern-inspired cocktails such as the Resurgens (peach-infused rye, sweet vermouth and house-made cola bitters) by mixologist Greg Best.

Trois
1180 Peachtree St.
404-815-3337
In addition to a refined lounge focused on classic and sparkling-wine cocktails, this three-story French restaurant has original art in its second-floor dining room.

AUSTIN

The Belmont
305 W. Sixth St.
512-457-0300
This retro restaurant and bar evokes Rat Pack–era Palm Springs; the furniture in its Vegas-style space is covered with acres of tufted leather, and its upstairs terrace has views of the Austin skyline.

BOSTON AREA

Craigie on Main
853 Main St., Cambridge
617-497-5511
The emphasis at this family-run bistro is on seasonal ingredients, both in chef Tony Maws's kitchen and in bar manager Tom Schlesinger-Guidelli's drinks. The vodka-based Hunter's Moon, for instance, is made with a spiced puree of local Musque de Provence winter squash.

Drink
348 Congress St., Boston
617-695-1806
A new venture from star chef Barbara Lynch, Drink dispenses with menus; mixologist John Gertsen and his team (who helped make the elegant bar at No. 9 Park one of the city's best) custom-make drinks for each customer.

Eastern Standard Kitchen & Drinks
528 Commonwealth Ave. Boston
617-532-9100
Jackson Cannon presides over Eastern Standard's marble-

topped bar (and the menu of 50-plus drinks) in Kenmore Square's Hotel Commonwealth.

Green Street
280 Green St., Cambridge
617-876-1655
The bar in this revamped Depression-era restaurant serves great vintage and modern cocktails.

Lobby Bar & Kitchen
131 Broad St., Boston
617-261-5353
This popular after-work spot in Boston's Financial District holds spirits tastings on Tuesday nights and serves signature drinks like Liquid Jailtime: strawberry-infused cachaça with muddled pink peppercorns.

RumBa
InterContinental Boston
510 Atlantic Ave., Boston
617-217-5752
The InterContinental's in-house lounge (with a drink list by Francesco Lafranconi) has a great selection of rums, Latin music and a velvet-banquetted Champagne bar.

CHICAGO

C-House
Affinia Chicago
166 E. Superior St.
312-523-0923
Star chef Marcus Samuelsson's refined fish house and chophouse has an extensive raw bar and cocktails that tend toward the sweet, like the Honey B (vodka, alfalfa honey and chamomile syrup).

The Drawing Room
937 N. Rush St.
312-266-2694
At this subterranean lounge within Le Passage nightclub, guests can opt to have their drinks prepared tableside, accompanied by a cocktail history lesson.

Green Mill
4802 N. Broadway
773-878-5552
A Chicago landmark (Al Capone purportedly hung out here), this renovated Uptown jazz club evokes the thirties and forties but features jazz from all eras.

Nacional 27
325 W. Huron St.
312-664-2727
Mixologist Adam Seger (who created the Frozen Drinks chapter, p. 80) makes the superfresh cocktails (both frozen and otherwise) at this Latin-inspired salsa club and restaurant.

The Violet Hour
1520 N. Damen Ave.
773-252-1500
This lounge is modeled after early-19th-century English clubs and French salons, complete with chandeliers and a fireplace. Floor-to-ceiling curtains frame the bartenders as if they were on a stage.

CLEVELAND

The Velvet Tango Room
2095 Columbus Rd.
216-241-8869
A piano player accompanies the clinking of perfectly square ice cubes at this swank, living room–like cocktail purists' hangout.

DENVER & BOULDER

Frasca Food & Wine
1738 Pearl St., Boulder
303-442-6966
Master sommelier Bobby Stuckey and überchef Lachlan Mackinnon-Patterson's Friulian restaurant specializes in Italian aperitifs and digestifs.

The Kitchen [Upstairs]
1039 Pearl St., Boulder
303-544-5973
This comfortable lounge above The Kitchen has a terrific selection of spirits (like Leopold Bros. Absinthe Verte) and hosts a daily "tasting hour" of affordable small plates and seasonal drinks.

Steuben's Food Service
523 East 17th Ave. Denver
303-830-1001
A reimagined version of the classic American chrome-and-comfort-food diner, Steuben's serves bacon-infused-vodka Bloody Marys as well as Monte Cristos and fries.

The West End Tavern
926 Pearl St., Boulder
303-444-3535
An updated American tavern, the West End offers an amazing selection of bourbons at its antique wooden bar and on its rooftop patio overlooking the Flatirons.

EUGENE, OR

Bel Ami Restaurant & Lounge
Midtown Marketplace
1591 Willamette St.
541-485-6242
Bel Ami has an impressive collection of spirits, particularly American whiskey, plus concoctions like East of Eden (gin, lemon and an Oregon Pinot Gris reduction).

HONOLULU

RumFire
Sheraton Waikiki
2255 Kalakaua Ave.
808-922-4422
Mixologist Francesco Lafranconi created drinks for this rum-centric Euro-Pacific tapas spot, which pours more than 100 labels of its namesake spirit.

HOUSTON

Backstreet Café
1103 S. Shepherd Dr.
713-521-2239
The tree-shaded patio of this New American restaurant is as big a draw as the cocktails. These include daily-changing sangrias and the Forty-Year-Old Milkshake (a mix of honey, mascarpone ice cream and sherry).

Beaver's
2310 Decatur St.
713-864-2328
Located in a former icehouse, Beaver's maintains the tradition of these casual eating-and-drinking spots with easy-drinking "Front Porch" cocktails, "beer-tails" and terrific slow-cooked barbecue.

KANSAS CITY, MO

Jp Wine Bar
1526 Walnut St.
816-842-2660
This Crossroads district coffee and wine bar also serves great wine-based cocktails

like the Americana (bourbon, blood orange bitters, peaches and sparkling wine).

The Oak Bar
InterContinental Kansas City at the Plaza
401 Ward Pkwy.
816-756-1500
This refined bar connected to the Oak Room restaurant has a working fireplace (which gives it a social-club feel), a martini-focused drink list and a cabinet of cigars.

LAS VEGAS

Downtown Cocktail Room
111 Las Vegas Blvd. South
702-880-3696
This spacious and subdued lounge in a renovated wedding chapel is marked by a tiny sign; inside are cool drinks like the Cat's Pajamas (gin, Campari, orange juice, Chartreuse and maple syrup).

Fontana Bar
Bellagio
3600 Las Vegas Blvd. South
702-693-7089
Fontana Bar has live music, a huge range of drinks and a patio overlooking the Bellagio's famous eight-acre lake full of "dancing fountains."

Nora's Cuisine
6020 W. Flamingo Rd.
702-873-8990
This family-run restaurant is a favorite with locals for its hearty Italian menu and old-school cocktails like Negronis and sidecars.

Rosemary's Restaurant
8125 W. Sahara Ave.
702-869-2251
The husband-and-wife chef team at this cozy restaurant serves great small plates (like veal sweetbreads over heirloom grits) and a mix of updated and classic cocktails, such as Yuzu Margaritas and Brandy Alexanders.

LOS ANGELES AREA

Bar Centro
The Bazaar, SLS Hotel at Beverly Hills
465 S. La Cienega Blvd. Los Angeles
310-246-5555
This surrealist-chic lounge—complete with a fortune teller—is part of superchef José Andrés's new culinary center (which includes the restaurant Rojo y Blanca). Avant-garde drinks are made with ingredients like liquid nitrogen, cotton candy and "olive brine air."

Comme Ça
8479 Melrose Ave. West Hollywood
323-782-1104
Star chef David Myers of Sona has created a modern brasserie, complete with Parisian staples (*steak frites*) and updated retro cocktails like the Gin & Tarragonic.

Copa d'Oro
217 Broadway Santa Monica
310-576-3030
This brand-new bar headed by Vincenzo Marianella has a

"be your own mixologist" option. This allows guests to concoct their own drinks with seasonal ingredients (kumquats or sage, for instance) and a choice of artisanal spirits.

The Doheny
714 West Olympic Blvd.
Los Angeles
No phone; thedoheny.com
Vincenzo Marianella created cocktails for this exclusive, invitation-only club, which has a list of 25 cocktails and a smoking area inside a former greenhouse.

The Edison
108 W. Second St.
Los Angeles
213-613-0000
This lounge inside an early 1900s power plant serves handcrafted cocktails, an amazing selection of gins and snacks like lobster-sausage corn dogs with mustard crème fraîche.

The Hungry Cat
1535 Vine St., Hollywood
323-462-2155
Made with local vegetables and herbs, the Hungry Cat's Holy Mary (vodka, fresh juices from carrot, lemon and ginger, plus rosemary and parsley) is terrific with chef David Lentz's burgers, seafood and raw bar.

Musso & Frank Grill
6667 Hollywood Blvd.
Hollywood
323-467-7788
The cocktail and food menus (and the bow-tied waiters) at Hollywood's oldest restaurant have remained virtually unchanged since the place opened in 1919. The Silver Screen clientele, however, has been replaced by actors like Brad Pitt.

The Penthouse
The Huntley Hotel
1111 Second St.
Santa Monica
310-393-8080
Star mixologist Ryan Magarian developed the drink list at this luxurious 18th-floor restaurant and lounge, which has fantastic views of the Pacific Ocean and Hollywood.

Seven Grand
515 W. Seventh St.
Los Angeles
213-614-0737
One part Irish pub, one part English hunting lodge, this hip second-floor lounge serves 125 whiskeys.

The Varnish
118 E. Sixth St.
Los Angeles
213-622-4090
A collaboration between cocktail heroes Sasha Petraske and Eric Alperin, the Varnish is accessible only through a secret door at the newly renovated Cole's, downtown L.A.'s century-old public house (a.k.a. saloon).

MADISON, WI

Maduro
117 E. Main St.
608-294-9371
Smoking of cigars and pipes (but not cigarettes) is welcome here. Maduro has a rotating selection of stogies, an extensive spirits list and cocktails like the Ipanema (cachaça, Licor 43 and orange and lime juices).

Natt Spil
211 King St.
No phone
In an unassuming building, this perpetually busy restaurant is known for DJ-spun music and original concoctions like the Créole Napoleon (rum, muddled ginger and the spicy orange liqueur Créole Shrubb).

MIAMI BEACH

The Florida Room
Delano Hotel
1685 Collins Ave.
305-674-6152
The center of Miami Beach nightlife, Lenny Kravitz's updated 1950s Cuban–style lounge has live music (played on a Lucite grand piano) and Latin-inspired drinks.

MINNEAPOLIS

Bradstreet Craftshouse Restaurant
Graves 601 Hotel
601 First Ave. North
612-312-1821
This new restaurant has a drink menu by Toby Maloney and a private "parlour room" hidden behind a velvet curtain.

La Belle Vie
510 Groveland Ave.
612-874-6440
At this elegant French-Mediterranean restaurant's candle-lit lounge, bartender Johnny Michaels honors *la belle vie* with cocktails like the Bronco Nagurski (rye whiskey and house-made root beer bitters).

NEW HAMPSHIRE

White Mountain Cider Co.
Rte. 302, Glen
603-383-9061
Jeff Grdinich, creator of the After-Dinner Drinks chapter (p. 106), manages the bar at this farmhouse restaurant. A store next door sells some of the syrups and bitters used at the bar.

NEW JERSEY

Catherine Lombardi Restaurant
3 Livingston Ave.
New Brunswick
732-296-9463
Old-school cocktails like the Bee's Knees and Brooklyn-influenced Neapolitan dishes are the heart of this restaurant and bar.

NEW ORLEANS

Arnaud's French 75 Bar
813 Rue Bienville
504-523-5433
This dapper, cigar-friendly bar is inside Arnaud's, one of New Orleans's oldest and most venerated restaurants.

Bar UnCommon
Renaissance Pere Marquette Hotel
817 Common St.
504-525-1111
Fourth-generation bartender Chris McMillian creates classic-inspired cocktails like ginger-spiked Manhattans at this stylish bar.

Café Adelaide & The Swizzle Stick Bar
Loews New Orleans Hotel
300 Poydras St.
504-595-3305
Named for the now-deceased bon vivant Adelaide Brennan, this café and bar celebrates fifties and sixties cocktail culture.

Carousel Piano Bar & Lounge
Hotel Monteleone
214 Rue Royale
504-523-3341
One of New Orleans's most famous watering holes, this circus-themed piano bar has a carousel on its revolving bar.

Cochon
930 Tchoupitoulas St.
504-588-2123
Star chef Donald Link's pork-centric Cajun restaurant serves traditional Southern cocktails like Sazeracs and mint juleps, small-batch bourbons and a selection of moonshine (i.e., corn whiskey).

Commander's Palace
1403 Washington Ave.
504-899-8221
Celebrity chef Emeril Lagasse made his name at this genteel, Victorian-style, classic Creole restaurant in the Garden District. Open since 1880, it's a great place for old-school cocktails like Sazeracs and Ramos Gin Fizzes.

Napoleon House
500 Chartres St.
504-524-9752
A local institution, this shabbily elegant restaurant and bar has a Spanish-style courtyard, plays classical music and is known for its Pimm's Cups and muffuletta sandwiches.

NEW YORK CITY

Apothéke
9 Doyers St., Manhattan
212-406-0400
This Chinatown "cocktail apothecary" has more than 250 specialty drinks created with house-made liqueurs and infusions. Their "Pain Killers" feature ingredients like tequila and peppery spices, while their "Health and Beauty" drinks use ingredients like rose water.

B Flat
277 Church St.
Manhattan
212-219-2970
This subterranean lounge has live jazz, excellent Asian-influenced small plates and cocktails named after jazz classics like "Giant Steps."

Brandy Library
25 N. Moore St.
Manhattan
212-226-5545
Home to one of the most extensive Scotch lists in New York City, Brandy Library offers more than 900 spirits and 100 cocktails.

Clover Club
210 Smith St.
Brooklyn
718-855-7939
This new classics–focused venture is co-owned by Julie Reiner of Manhattan's renowned Flatiron Lounge. She created the drinks in the Mocktails chapter (p. 148).

Death & Co.
433 E. Sixth St.
Manhattan
212-388-0882
Joaquin Simo, who created the drinks for the Latin Drinks chapter (p. 48), and the other vest-clad bartenders at this East Village spot have an encyclopedic knowledge of cocktails.

Dutch Kills
27-24 Jackson Ave.
Queens
718-383-2724
Modeled after an 1890s "gentleman's tavern," the newest bar from local hero mixologist Richard Boccato serves classic cocktails made with hand-cut ice and pub food from the local Sage General Store. A band performs jazz and ragtime standards.

Employees Only
510 Hudson St.
Manhattan
212-242-3021
This bartender-owned supper club was originally intended to be a late-night gathering spot for fellow bar and restaurant workers.

Little Branch
22 Seventh Ave. South
Manhattan
212-929-4360
This West Village basement lounge is owned by über-mixologist Joseph Schwartz. Drinks are served with ice that's custom-made for each glass.

Milk & Honey
134 Eldridge St.
Manhattan
No phone
An unlisted phone number and an entrance policy that requires a referral and an appointment make this flagship Sasha Petraske spot one of Manhattan's most exclusive lounges.

PDT
113 St. Marks Pl.
Manhattan
212-614-0386
Mixologist Jim Meehan, who compiled the recipes for both the Classics (p. 118) and Mixologists' Drinks chapters (p. 132), presides over this reservations-only lounge. It's unmarked and entered through a phone booth tucked inside the hot dog joint Crif Dogs.

Pegu Club
77 W. Houston St.
Manhattan
212-473-7348
Vintage cocktail connoisseur Audrey Saunders co-owns this mixologists' hangout, which serves its cocktails with dropper bottles filled with fresh juices, Angostura bitters and simple syrup.

Prime Meats
465 Court St.,
Brooklyn
718-254-0327
Owners Frank Castronovo and Frank Falcinelli of Frankies 457 Spuntino toured breweries in Munich for inspiration before opening their new spot. It consists of a barroom, an upstairs speakeasy and a main dining room.

Rayuela

165 Allen St., Manhattan
212-253-8840
This pan-Latin spot serves traditional sangrias and mojitos as well as *estilo libre* ("freestyle") cocktails. These combine unexpected ingredients like ginger, jicama, pineapple and mezcal.

Tailor

525 Broome St.
Manhattan
212-334-5182
Bartender and experimentalist Eben Freeman and chef avant-gardist Sam Mason (both formerly of wd-50) are the duo behind this cocktail destination.

PHILADELPHIA

APO Bar & Lounge

102 S. 13th St.
215-735-7500
Tad Carducci and Paul Tanguay designed the menu at APO (known to locals as Apothecary). Drinks in the "Elixirs" section have tongue-in-cheek names like Tippling Bros. Magical Pain Extractor (made with mint, rosemary, cayenne extract and Sicilian amaro).

Chick's Cafe

614 S. Seventh St.
215-625-3700
Recently restored by its new owners, Chick's maintains the original pressed-tin ceiling and cherry bar, and features great classic-inspired cocktails.

Southwark

701 S. Fourth St.
215-238-1888
This corner restaurant and barroom offers old-school cocktails and an impressive selection of ryes and gins.

Tequila's Restaurant

1602 Locust St.
215-546-0181
At his elegant hacienda-style restaurant, David Suro, who grew up near agave fields in the Mexican state of Jalisco, serves drinks by mixologist Junior Merino and around 100 tequilas.

PORTLAND, OR

Andina

1314 NW Glisan St.
503-228-9535
At this Peruvian restaurant's Bar Mestizo, the Nuevo Latino and classic Latin cocktails (like a top-shelf pisco sour) are accompanied every night by live jazz, Latin or swing music.

Clyde Common

1014 SW Stark St.
503-228-3333
Communal seating defines this airy, industrial "tavern." It has inspired small plates (popcorn with pimentón) and fantastic cocktails like the Ivy League (bourbon, cherry brandy and green walnut liqueur).

Red Star

503 SW Alder St.
503-222-0005
Along with bar snacks like rock shrimp hushpuppies, Red Star has a great selection of single-malt Scotches and small-batch bourbons. Its menu showcases bourbon cocktails.

Teardrop Cocktail Lounge
1015 NW Everett St.
503-445-8109
The detail-obsessed bartenders at this Pearl District destination make their own bitters, tonic water and specialty liqueurs. One night a month they feature drinks from a vintage cocktail book.

Ten 01
1001 NW Couch St.
503-226-3463
Creations like a celery-spiked gin fizz and more than 200 spirits complement chef Jack Yoss's seasonal New American bar snacks. These include a tasty chorizo burger with pickled shallots and a fried egg.

SAN FRANCISCO AREA

Absinthe Brasserie & Bar
398 Hayes St.
San Francisco
415-551-1590
Francophiles crowd the copper-topped tables at this San Francisco institution. The draw: stellar cocktails and brasserie-style dishes from *Top Chef* Season 5 contestant Jamie Lauren.

The Alembic
1725 Haight St.
San Francisco
415-666-0822
This gastropub has lists of "After-Dinner Libations," which include a carefully curated selection of brandies and grappas, and "Daytime" drinks like Bloody Marys and mint juleps.

Beretta
1199 Valencia St.
San Francisco
415-695-1199
Mission District newcomer Beretta is an upscale pizzeria with communal seating and a late-night cocktail lounge that serves drinks designed by star mixologist Thad Vogler.

Bix
56 Gold St.
San Francisco
415-433-6300
This supper club evokes the ambience of Cunard ships from the thirties and forties with classic drinks, a massive spirits selection and live jazz every night.

Bourbon & Branch
501 Jones St.
San Francisco
415-673-1921
Bourbon & Branch occupies the space where an actual speakeasy operated during Prohibition.

Cantina
580 Sutter St.
San Francisco
415-398-0195
Duggan McDonnell's Latin-inspired lounge features rotating art exhibits and eccentric cocktails. Many of his creations are featured in the Pitcher Drinks chapter (p. 94).

Clock Bar
The Westin St. Francis
335 Powell St.
San Francisco
415-397-9222
The St. Francis claims to be the birthplace of the olive-garnished martini. Restaurateur Michael Mina's new bar serves this drink, which they call the St. Francis Cocktail, as well as other classics.

Elixir

3200 16th St.
San Francisco
415-552-1633
H. Joseph Ehrmann creates drinks at this refurbished saloon with seasonal fruit juices, house-made mixers and spirits from Bay Area distillers like Hangar One and No. 209.

Forbidden Island

1304 Lincoln Ave.
Alameda
510-749-0332
This sixties-style tiki lounge makes almost every tropical drink, from Trader Vic's mai tai to the Suffering Bastard from Cairo's Shepheard's Hotel.

Heaven's Dog

1148 Mission St.
San Francisco
415-863-6008
This new Chinese noodle bar and lounge from chef Charles Phan of the Slanted Door offers a dozen or so classically influenced cocktails from Erik Adkins, like the Pan American Clipper (Calvados, absinthe and local grenadine). Other mixologists will soon contribute to the changing drink menu.

Nopa

560 Divisadero St.
San Francisco
415-864-8643
Star mixologist Neyah White serves his own home-finished Red Head rye whiskey (aged in Zinfandel barrels) at this late-night neighborhood gathering place.

Range

842 Valencia St.
San Francisco
415-282-8283
The bartenders at this buzzing Mission District restaurant are known for their inventive seasonal cocktails, made with everything from kumquat and sage to grapefruit and vanilla.

The Slanted Door

1 Ferry Building #3
San Francisco
415-861-8032
At the Slanted Door, many of the cocktails (like the Ginger Limeade—kaffir lime vodka, ginger and lime juice) are designed to complement chef Charles Phan's modern Vietnamese menu.

SEATTLE

ART Lounge

Four Seasons Hotel
99 Union St.
206-749-7070
This modern hotel bar near the Seattle Art Museum has bar snacks like truffled beef tartare and drinks like the Big Dill (vodka, lime juice, agave nectar and dill), plus great views of Elliot Bay.

Licorous

928 12th Ave.
206-325-6947
Chef Johnathan Sundstrom's seasonally minded restaurant pairs its drinks with food. The Pharmacists' Cocktail (orange-infused gin, Pimm's, Lillet and house-made bitters), for example, goes with duck rillettes and cherry chutney.

Sun Liquor
607 Summit Ave. East
206-860-1130
This candlelit Capitol Hill bar focuses on classic cocktails, particularly whiskey and rum drinks. The furniture is made from refurbished wood.

Tini Bigs
100 Denny Way
206-284-0931
This self-proclaimed "Scotch and martini and cigar bar" has a 100-year-old wooden bar and a revamped drink menu by Jamie Boudreau, who created the Aperitifs chapter (p. 32).

Vessel
1312 Fifth Ave.
206-652-0521
Craftsmanship is the focus at this elegant, modern bar in a renovated 1920s building. Cocktail aesthetes come for rum swizzles and marmalade sours.

Zig Zag Café
1501 Western Ave.
206-625-1146
This bartender-owned café and bar near Pike Place Market serves forgotten drinks from old cocktail guides, like the Tipperary (Irish whiskey, vermouth and green Chartreuse).

ST. LOUIS

Monarch
7401 Manchester Rd.
314-644-3995
Mixologist and bar manager Ted Kilgore takes his cues from both pre- and post-Prohibition-era cocktails when inventing drinks like his Revival (rye, Bénédictine and maraschino liqueur).

WASHINGTON, DC, AREA

Bar Pilar
1833 14th St. NW
202-265-1751
At this terrific food-and-drink spot, bar manager Adam Bernbach hosts a "cocktail session" every Tuesday, featuring five of his original seasonal drinks, which use obscure spirits like Barolo Chinato.

Café Atlántico
405 Eighth St. NW
Washington, DC
202-393-0812
Traditional and evolved versions of mojitos and caipirinhas accompany the Nuevo Latino menu at star chef José Andrés's colorful multilevel restaurant.

The Gibson
2009 14th St. NW
Washington, DC
202-232-2156
This exclusive bar with a no-standing policy is all about well-crafted cocktails, both classic and innovative. The waitstaff flames twists over drinks tableside.

PX
728 King St.
Alexandria, VA
703-299-8385
Todd Thrasher, who created the Seasonal Drinks chapter (p. 64), makes the cocktails at this chandelier-dotted speakeasy (there's no sign outside, just a blue light). It's owned by the team behind the terrific Restaurant Eve.

drinks & spirits index

H

L

M

N

O

P

R

T

V

W

party-food index

Châtelaine, p. 35

"Manhattan" cocktail glass by Theresienthal.

thank you

This collection of cocktails would not have been possible without the help of these people.

Eric Alperin
Greg Best
Jacques Bezuidenhout
Greg Boehm
Jamie Boudreau
Derek Brown
Jackson Cannon
Tad Carducci
Alex Day
Eben Freeman
Avery & Janet Glasser
Jeff Grdinich
Chris Hannah
Mike Henderson
Ben Jones
Misty Kalkofen
Ted Kilgore
Francesco Lafranconi
John Lermayer
Katie Loeb
Ryan Magarian
Toby Maloney
Vincenzo Marianella
Duggan McDonnell
Brian Miller
Jeffrey Morgenthaler
Jonny Raglin
Julie Reiner
Sam Ross
Adam Seger
Daniel Shoemaker
Marcos Tello
Todd Thrasher
Philip Ward
Thomas Waugh
Neyah White
Rhea Wong

More books from

FOOD & WINE

Best of the Best

The best recipes from the 25 best cookbooks of the year

Annual Cookbook 2009

An entire year of recipes

Wine Guide 2009

The most up-to-date guide, with more than 1,000 recommendations